Less Ketchup

Than Salsa

Finding My Mojo

in Travel Writing

Joe Cawley

ISBN-13: 9781717710420

For my eternal sunshine, Joy, my moonlight Molly Blue, and my shining star, Sam.

Also written in loving memory of my dear Mum and Nan. RIP.

Acknowledgments

Big thanks to my family for putting up with my dizzy-headiness and blank stares when they try to have a conversation with me and my mind is on writing.

Also to my editor, Lucy Ridout, whose black belt in word-wrangling helped corral this story from a gibbering wreck into some kind of cohesion.

Tenerife

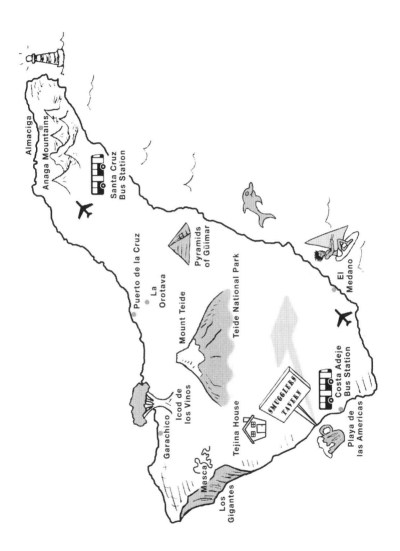

CHAPTER ONE

'Surprise!'

Joy's face was as blank as mine.

'Remember us?' said the lady standing in our apartment doorway. Her bingo wings jiggled as she held up outstretched hands bejewelled in rose gold.

Joy smiled, without commitment.

The lady raised her drawn-on eyebrows, turned her head slightly and waited for the penny to drop. It didn't. She tried jazz hands. That didn't free the penny either.

Her husband stood stiffly, a full pace further back, hands behind his back. His mouth was fixed in a manic grin, the type you inadvertently do when your lips are dry and get stuck to your gums. 'Stan. And Vera,' he said, like a ventriloquist's dummy.

'Ah!' said Joy. 'Half a shandy; gin, Indian tonic.'

I dutifully smiled and nodded as if I had a clue. Joy always remembered ex-customers by what they'd habitually drunk.

'Babs at timeshare reception told us where you lived,' smiled Gin Indian Tonic (we'll call her GIT for the sake of brevity, and because she was one). GIT strode purposefully into our apartment.

'Oh, right,' said Joy, trying to sound pleased.

I made a mental note to shoot Babs in the knee.

'Nice,' said GIT, looking round. 'Small, but nice. Easy to clean...' She stroked a finger across the top bar of a pine chair. '... you'd think.'

Shandy remained rooted in the doorway. He continued grinning, as though this was part of a viable conversation, dentures still clenched and showing.

'Listen,' I said, turning my head to address them both, 'I have no idea who you are. Clearly, you're not our friends, and even more clearly, you're both slightly deranged. We have a hundred other things that we'd rather be doing than making polite conversation with you two, so pack your bags, sling your hook and close the door behind you.'

That's what I'd have liked to have said. What I actually said was, 'Can I get you a drink? Tea, coffee, wine?'

Twelve months on and we still couldn't shake off the ghost of Smugglers. Joy and I had survived seven years of pandering to the bewildered, deranged and downright demanding patrons of our pub in Tenerife. At least that's what it had felt like at times. Having stumbled along a crazy-paved path of self-discovery and frequent self-destruction, we had progressed from fish-stall workers to successful expat publicans, and although our life behind bars had now come to an end, sticky crumbs from our erstwhile career resurfaced in awkward places.

Those with whom we'd chosen to sustain an acquaintance

in Tenerife still expected us to act the happy hosts during meals out. And why not? It was a role they'd repeatedly paid to see us play for seven years and now that we'd moved from our familiar venue we were simply viewed as a touring panto.

It wasn't *all* the fault of others. Our years of conditioning were hard to shake. Sometimes it wasn't the people but the environment that triggered a Pavlovian response and soured the sweet novelty of freedom. A return to a familiar setting risked stirring the subconscious with sights, smells or sounds that we associated with time-sensitive tasks. Wine-addled seafood lunches at fishing-village restaurants in La Caleta or Los Abrigos would be haunted by the fear of deadlines missed: 'Don't you have cucumbers to prep before customers arrive?'

My mind could be put in a flurry by the mere sight of a Caesar salad: 'Did you buy enough lettuce today?' Even a visit to the urinals could prompt a mental note to set to with a scouring pad and bleach, and more than once I had to stop myself from picking cigarette butts and chewing gum out of the bowl.

Despite our post-traumatic-stress disorder, we had a lot going for us. Our relationship had survived a near-fatal shattering and remained intact, we had more money in the bank than we currently knew what to do with, and we were free to get up at hours that suited us and dally with the day however we desired. It was bliss. But an uncomfortable bliss, if there can be such a thing.

Although Whim had been the main driving force behind our move to Tenerife in 1991, I was older now, and wiser, I liked to think. I'd realised Whim was not to be trusted. That mischievous imp had very nearly landed us in the proverbial poop. Or Llandudno, to be precise. Fortunately, Sense had stepped in at the last hour and slapped us about the head, and we narrowly avoided moving from frying pan to fryer following Whim's insistence that running a bed-and-breakfast in north Wales was our future.

However, we did agree on one thing with Whim – we, or rather I, definitely needed to do something. But what?

Aimlessness has its place, a by-product of passivity in those content to drift wherever the current takes them. That had been me eight years ago, but it wasn't me now. Having the Smugglers had instilled in me if not a sense of urgency at least the realisation that idling in an ocean-facing bungalow at thirty-four years of age was not where I wanted to be. New adventures were not going to unfurl before me; I would have to go and find them.

Repelling land assaults by Shandy and GIT were not the adventures I had in mind. It took two hours of banal conversation before we could peel them off our settee and usher them out the door.

'It's been lovely. I'm so glad we found you. We'll call round again soon,' threatened GIT.

We waved them off with professional smiles and thoughts of moving. Whim suggested murder. Whim had its uses.

Unfortunately, GIT and Shandy weren't our only unexpected visitors following our Smugglers retirement, but they were by far the most persistent, blessing us with their presence at least once a fortnight during their three-month stays in Tenerife. In El Beril we were sitting targets, especially as we did very little during the day other than spend time together in the apartment.

Despite our inertia, three big events happened in the year 2000 (four if you include the Y2K millennium bug that was going to stop the world but didn't). One involved the pitter-patter of tiny feet and one would finally foil the plans of people like Shandy and GIT, but it was the third that would alter the course of my life for ever.

CHAPTER TWO

We were curled up on the sofa watching daytime TV in our apartment.

'Turn the telly down a minute.' Joy tilted her head to one side, listening.

I grabbed the remote control from the glass coffee table. There was nothing at first, then a tiny scratching.

'Damn, mice again,' I said.

'That's not a mouse. It's coming from behind the patio curtains. Go have a look.'

I squinted into a landscape bleached by blistering sunlight. 'Can't see any— Oh! Hang on.' I slid open the patio door and scooped up a tiny white bundle. The high-pitched complaining ceased for a moment as it sunk small claws into my palm and bared its teeth.

'Ouch!' I lowered the kitten carefully onto the marble floor of our living room. The mewing started up again and the blob of fluff began to sway and shake as if it was experiencing its own little earthquake.

'Aww,' cooed Joy. 'I think it's hungry. Give it some milk and a bit of that ham.'

'Whoa, whoa, whoa.' I held a hand up. 'If we feed it now, that's it. It's ours. It'll never leave.'

'Well, you can't let it starve. Look at it, poor thing, it's shaking with hunger. So cute!'

Cute it wasn't. The kitten continued to vibrate at a steady rate of knots. I picked it up again and the shaking stopped. It looked like the kind of kitten a three-year-old would draw long before any sense of perspective had taken hold. Huge eyes bulged from a head blotchy with angry red scabs. At the other end, a thin pipe-cleaner of a tail protruded from its bloated pink body.

'Got a skin infection,' I said, holding it at eye level. 'Ew. And worms.' I jerked my head back as it took a quick swipe at my nose. 'Still got some fight left in him though.' I turned him around. 'Her,' I corrected.

In addition to its skin affliction, the kitten's eyes were clogged with grey-green pus, and a thin trickle of mucous hung from its button nose. It was, by some distance, the ugliest kitten I had ever seen. Despite that, it seemed there was no going back. It devoured several slices of ham and two saucers of milk, then brought it all back up again in a series of gooey convulsions.

'We should call it Elvis,' said Joy.

I looked bemused.

'Shakes its hips like Elvis Presley – look.'

'Or Fugly,' I offered. 'Flaming ugly.' And so it became. Our fist offspring was officially named Fugly, an ugly duckling that grew into a beautiful swan. Only she didn't, but more of that later.

Over the coming days, Fugly bonded with Joy to the point of my exclusion. I was under the impression that new-born orphaned animals attached themselves with fierce loyalty to the first creature they interacted with. *I* had picked her up. *I* had examined her. *I* had fed her ham and milk and cleaned up the sick, but it was Joy who was the chosen one. It was she who was seen as the carer, the one to sit near but not on – the kitten was still building trust in that area. Despite Joy's admonishment to 'stop being soft', I felt snubbed.

Not only was I not seen as her saviour, I was now viewed as the enemy, though I did gain some comfort in knowing that I was not alone – cushions, errant shoes, the sweeping brush, curtains that swished, shopping bags and anything else that dared to exist, living or inanimate, were all objects of Fugly's hostility. In fact, everything except Joy.

What she lacked in looks, Fugly more than made up for in psychotic tendencies. If a stranger walked past our patio, her eyes would snap to the target like the blade of a flick-knife. If the passer-by carried on walking, they were safe. If they paused to peer inside our apartment, their curiosity would turn to terror as a spitting, snarling, white ball of fluff charged towards them.

At first I was irritated by this paranoid behaviour, but I warmed to it slightly when I witnessed how Fugly's narkiness could be turned to our advantage.

'Oh, how sweet, you have a cat!' said GIT as she strode past us and through the doorway during her next invasion of our home. She bent low to stroke Fugly.

Never one to miss the chance to inflict pain, our kitten sank her tiny razor teeth into GIT's forefinger. At the same time, three lines of blood appeared on the back of GIT's hand, courtesy of a raking claw.

'Fugly!' I shouted, trying to hide my fatherly pride.

Joy passed GIT a piece of kitchen roll.

'Not very friendly, is he?' said GIT.

'She's a she. Doesn't like unexpected visitors,' I said pointedly. And the moment would have passed. Except Fugly wasn't done.

When Shandy sat down, Fugly leapt onto the back of the settee and lashed out Zorro-like at the nape of his neck. Shandy sprang to his feet as if he'd sat on a nail. GIT emerged from the bathroom having washed the blood off her hand and crossed paths with her husband, who was hurrying to the sink.

'What happened?' She turned to him, but before he could answer, Fugly attacked hard and low, scratching at varicose veins and biting fat, turquoise-painted toes.

'What the heck is wrong with that thing!' shrieked GIT as she performed a defensive cancan.

Joy scooped up Fugly and locked her in the bedroom. 'Sorry about that. She gets a little excited when we have company.'

'Excited! You need to have her put down. She could have rabies or something. Have you got any plasters?'

We did, but I pretended we didn't, which seemed to do the trick. Our unwanted guests departed, muttering something about tetanus, irresponsible owners and calling the police. Finally, we were left in peace. For now.

CHAPTER THREE

Joy was halfway up a stepladder with a can of crimson emulsion by her side. She hummed refrains from a Michael Bolton album that had been subliminally implanted in her brain during our Smugglers days. I knelt at her feet, tongue protruding from the side of my mouth, meticulously painting along the top of a marble skirting board.

Both of us wore black T-shirts emblazoned with gold lettering: 'SMUGG' on the front, 'LERS' on the back. They were remnants from days gone by, plucked from a bin liner full of T-shirts that we'd had printed for bar customers.

Many in the black bin bag were special editions. Additional lettering listed both the date of our initial bar opening (June 1st, 1991) and the day of what was supposed to be our Smugglers leaving party (May 30th, 1998), after we'd sold the bar to a local 'godfather' of Italian descent and dubious background.

If you've followed the *Ketchup* saga from Book One, you'll know that this first sale fell through. Although we were left with a sizeable non-returnable deposit, we were also left with an overwhelming feeling of despair and a large bag of commemorative T-shirts. We still have some if you'd like one. Email me via the address at the back of the book and we can sort something out. They make very good painting smocks and/or cleaning rags.

Anyway, I digress... We had set about sprucing up the apartment – cleaning it, shuffling furniture around – in the hope that a change of immediate scenery would fill the hole in our lives.

Our seven-year bar career had been pitted with anguish and disasters – both professional and personal – but as well as providing an inordinate amount of cash, it had forced on us a resolute sense of purpose. We might have been bleary-eyed from continual nights of too-little sleep, but every day we woke knowing what had to be done. Our journey was plotted, the ship travelling under full sail. All we had to do was keep it on course.

Now we felt adrift, bobbing in an ocean of uncertainty. That might sound liberating, and in many ways it was. Everybody needs a little uncertainty in their lives, but it has to be counterbalanced with elements of predictability and structure and a rough sense of what *might* be coming. We didn't have a clue. So it was no great surprise that Michael Bolton and red paint didn't fill the gap.

As we stood back to survey our handiwork, we were satisfied that, aesthetically at least, the blandness had been eliminated. We were not so happy that it been replaced by hideousness.

'What do you think?' I asked, arms crossed, trying to find a single redeeming feature in our colour of choice.

'Looks vile,' said Joy cheerily.

The crimson made our apartment feel like a claustrophobic den of iniquity. We decided to revert to the original cream colour.

It was our second bout of decorating in less than a week. Because of the crimson disaster, we'd become quite adept at painting. 'We're getting good at this,' said Joy, as she thrust the paint roller up and down the wall. I felt another shower of paint splatter on my head. 'We could do this for a living.'

For no other reason than that we could think of nothing else to do, the notion stuck, and 'Painterman' business cards confirmed our new vocation.

Four months and a dozen jobs later, the Painterman sheen had faded. There had been no struggle to secure work; in fact, the novelty of a young, or by now youngish couple painting apartments together at a reasonable rate meant that word spread fast. The demand for our brush skills began to exceed supply.

Requests started coming in not only from private house owners but from business owners too. From one-bed apartments we moved on to four-bed villas, which involved renting, transporting and subsequently climbing long ladders to reach the higher ceilings, and getting drawn into conversations on topics that we knew nothing about. 'What product would you recommend we use on the covings?' or 'Could you give the bathroom walls a kind of stucco, stipple effect.'

Then I was asked to provide a quote at an apartment complex overlooking Puerto Colon harbour. The German community president was waiting for me in the car park. We shook hands, exchanged pleasantries in broken English, and got down to business.

'So, is it *your* apartment you'd like us to paint?' I said.

'Yes, my apartments,' said the president.

'Oh, apartments! You have more than one?'

'Yes, all my apartments.'

'How many do you want me to paint?'

'All of them.'

'But how many?'

'One hundred and fifty-two.' He waved an arm at the flaking four-storey block in front of us. 'Inside and out.'

I gulped.

'You give me good price, yes?'

I didn't give him any price, good or bad. The job entailed stripping and redecorating the public corridors, the outside walls, and all the apartment interiors. Although it would have been a golden ticket to the next level of our painting-and-decorating careers, it didn't sound like fun at all. Unless we took on extra help, we would need the best part of a year. I had seen Painterman as a stopgap, a moderately rewarding pastime that would do until the Next Big Idea came to mind. But this sounded like a business, with long-term commitment – responsibility!

Those two words again! This near encounter with those evil twins seemed to suck the enjoyment out of what we were doing. Joy and I had been having fun together *and* making a little money as a bonus. But now it was time for something else.

CHAPTER FOUR

There was another reason why I couldn't commit to such a full-on project right now. I'd received a call from my brother, David, in the UK. Nan was in hospital, having fallen for the second time in as many days. They didn't think there were any broken bones, but given that she was ninety-three, the hospital naturally wanted to keep her in for observation and to run a few checks.

It was three thirty in the afternoon when I reached Clitheroe. Daylight had already gone back to bed and a December wind whipped discarded newspapers and other paper rubbish into a frenzied twirl along Whalley Road. I stepped out of the taxi and let myself in to my nan's house.

Nothing had changed. Except Nan wasn't there, of course. The ceramic funfair trinkets were still on show in the glass cabinet. Most of the ornaments had fallen over, Nan being either too short-sighted or too disinterested to right them. The cabinet itself was also heading for a fall, its usual precarious angle now verging on the point of total topple.

I pondered trying to straighten it but remembered Nan's complaints at my last attempt. 'Leave it be. I like it like that. Besides, if it goes, it goes. It's its own silly fault.' That had seemingly been Nan's mantra throughout life, a Lancashire version of *qué será, será* – whatever will be, will be. Perhaps her ability to dismiss stressful situations with a mere shrug of the shoulders was why she'd reached the grand old age of ninety in relatively good health.

Physically she was a demon, still domestically agile in her morning uniform of faded blue day-coat and fluffy pink slippers, single-handedly throwing sodden bedsheets over the washing line strung across her back yard; still trudging up the steep, carpeted staircase, bedtime cocoa in hand, once 'that nice Alastair Stewart had said all there was to say' on ITV's ten o'clock news.

And until the last twelve months or so, Nan's mental capacity had also remained at a high level, partly due to her 'use it or lose it' philosophy regarding daily exercise for the brain cells. Sitting down anywhere in her house had nearly always been accompanied by the rustle of papers stuffed under cushions – pages from word-search puzzle books, neatly folded newspaper crosswords torn from the *Daily Express*, or, more recently, Sudoku challenges provided by her *Woman's Weekly* magazine subscription. But this time I noticed no such brain stimulants.

David had bought Nan a large-screen TV, which now stood in the centre of the room on a thinning hearth rug in front of the electric fire, just three feet from Nan's armchair. I pushed the ignite button on the fire to warm up the tiny room and noticed the plastic casing on the left side of the TV had begun to melt, so

I wheeled the TV back a few inches, out of reach of the artificial flames.

In addition to the gradual fading of her mental faculties and her eyesight, David had told me over the phone that Nan's ankles had started to swell and that the doctor wanted to give her injections to reduce the inflammation. Nan, of course, had refused, preferring to let nature take its course. Her inflated ankles may have been a contributing factor to her instability, but it was more than that that had caused her to fall, leaving her with bruises to her head and forearms. The doctor and David suspected she'd been blacking out. Nan's defence was that she'd merely been getting up too quickly, 'making me head giddy'.

I slept at Nan's house under the foot-high pile of quilts on her bed. The mattress had long lost its ability to support any weight and just collapsed in the middle with a soft sigh of resignation. It was the same mattress David and I had clambered onto when we were toddlers, snuggling up to Nan and her tales of Lancastrian hardship when she was young.

As we lay there having our hair stroked, we would sink into that state between wakefulness and sleep, our young imaginations fired by whispered narratives of her working life in cotton mills, munitions factories and school canteens. Those stories came back to me now as I drifted into a similarly carefree slumber.

Next morning I went to visit her in the hospital. 'There's nowt wrong with me,' she shouted from where she lay propped up against the pillows. Her hearing aid was at the side of her bed and the sheets were tucked tightly under her chin. 'I can't be doing with all these sick folk coughing and spluttering throughout the night.'

Husbands in overcoats sat forlornly beside the seven other beds in the ward, providing physical if not conversational company to their sick wives.

'The doctor will be round soon,' I said, handing Nan a bag of sweets.

'He's a darky,' bellowed Nan matter-of-factly while sucking on a Mint Ball.

'You can't say that these days, Nan.' I moved the visitor's chair nearer to the bed in the hope she'd stop shouting.

'Why not? He's a darky, and that's that,' she yelled. 'No point denying it. You can see it in his skin. Got them big lips, too. Did you bring liquorice?' She peered into the paper bag.

I smiled apologetically at the adjacent cubicle, where three generations of Pakistanis were listening avidly to our conversation.

David had already told me what the doctor had diagnosed: high blood pressure, angina, anaemia, prediabetes, kidney infection, and cataracts in both eyes. It was a formidable list, but Nan was a formidable lady. She'd already beaten off two cancers, lost her son and been widowed twice. She wasn't one to be mugged by a gang of lesser afflictions.

The doctor had insisted that Nan should stay in hospital for a few days, at least until they'd cleared up the kidney infection, addressed the anaemia and balanced her blood-sugar level. He'd also brought up Nan's mental state. He was worried that she was showing early signs of dementia, forgetting names and repeatedly asking, 'What's this hotel called again?' He was alarmed that she was still having to fend for herself at home.

Both David and I tried to convince him that it had always been a very fine line between sensibleness and absurdity when it came to our nan. She was never one for convention, preferring to do things her way and follow her own logic, however bizarre that seemed to others, such as when she'd packed her TV remote control on a visit to Tenerife 'so I don't miss *Coronation Street*'. However, we agreed to keep an eye on her and report back if things deteriorated.

That night, against a background of crooning karaoke kings in a Clitheroe pub, David and I discussed what we'd do if Nan really couldn't look after herself safely. He and his wife, Andi, lived in a two-storey house with an upstairs bathroom and a near-vertical staircase that even the most athletic of firemen would find challenging, so Nan moving in with them was a non-starter. Bringing her over to Tenerife was a definite option, though emigration to a subtropical climate would naturally have its own challenges for a nonagenarian. It wasn't off the cards just yet, but easier alternatives (for everyone) had to be explored first.

Nan's pride and dignity were part of what kept her independent and fit. Like all people in the twilight of their lives, Nan would play Pensioner Top Trumps at any opportunity. She was engaged in a game when I returned to the hospital the next day.

She was sitting by the side of the bed when I arrived, resplendent in Barbara Cartland make-up and a full armoury of pearls. She looked like a dignitary on a royal tour, only the bed she was visiting was empty. She was conversing with a new neighbour, a pensioner with a shock of white hair and lips painted blood red. I could see that the competition had begun.

'You look marvellous,' said the neighbour to my beaming nan.

'Not bad for ninety-three, eh?' Nan waited for a reaction.

'Ooh, you're nearly as old as my sister, Maureen. She's ninety-four,' said the neighbour.

One–nil. I could see Nan choosing which card to play next as she rolled her dentures from side to side.

'I've had cancer twice,' she blurted out – rather randomly, I thought.

'Fancy that! So have I! Where was yours?'

'Breast and throat. Had to have it removed.'

'Your throat?'

'No, me breast.'

'Oh, I had both mine taken off,' countered the neighbour proudly.

Two–nil.

Nan popped a Mint Ball in her mouth. It clacked agitatedly against her teeth, like a clock ticking down time.

'I still live by myself, don't I, Joe?' She'd decided to draw me into the game now.

I leant down and gave her a kiss. 'Hi, Nan.'

Nan held onto my shirt. 'She's got lady problems,' she said. 'Nowt serious like I have.' She turned up her nose to emphasise the point.

'Well, good for you, Eileen,' said the neighbour.

Nan's eyes lit up. Two–one.

The neighbour continued. 'Good on you and everything, but I wouldn't want to do that, live by myself. Malcolm, my son, built me a little bungalow in the grounds of his estate, next to his house, but I said, "Malcolm, why don't I just move in with you and Barbara and have done with it?" Much easier. It's like living in a posh hotel.' She put a finger over her mouth as if sharing a secret. 'They do *everything* for me. I let them. Makes them feel good, you know?'

Nan's accent rose a couple of social strata. 'Joe and David, my grandsons, are the same. They both want me to come and live in their houses. Joe's a very successful businessman in Spain. But I don't want to be a burden. 'Sides, if you haven't got your independence, what have you got?'

Two–two. And with the ball in the back of the net, Nan settled for a draw, blew the final whistle and blatantly turned her back on the neighbour.

Before I headed back to Tenerife, David and I checked out a nursing home close to Nan's house in Clitheroe. It was the only one that had a vacancy, 'though things can change daily, as I'm sure you'll appreciate,' said the lady at the other end of the phone.

There was an air of sadness and foreboding about the place. The bare branches of overhanging oak trees scratched at the clear blue sky like gnarled fingers in rigor mortis. Through one of the square windows of the dark, stone-walled building, a lady stared at the two of us in the car park. Her face was expressionless, her shoulders sagged. Was she looking down at a life left behind or had the cruel confusions of seniority clouded any such thought processes?

Great efforts had been made to brighten the doorstep flowerpots with vibrant colour, but the drooping stems had been defeated by the December frosts, or possibly by the suffocating air of melancholy. I rang the bell and blew into my hands for warmth.

After several bouts of hand-blowing, I rang again, but still nobody came. Through the glass pane I watched a resident shuffle along the threadbare carpet to the end of the hallway, pause, and then shuffle all the way back. I smiled at her through the glass, expecting the door to open, but she stared through us as if we were invisible.

There was a shout, a gentle hand on her shoulder, and she was slowly turned and steered away by a plump nurse in a dark blue uniform.

With the resident safely set on a new flight path, the nurse opened the door and we stepped in. 'Sorry, it's elevenses. Usual mayhem.' She rolled her eyes. 'You here to visit someone?'

We explained the situation and were put in a holding pattern in the hallway while she finished distributing tepid drinks and Rich Tea biscuits. A sparsely decorated Christmas tree at the bottom of the winding staircase was the only nod to the forthcoming festivities in what was otherwise a depressingly dreary scene. Worse than the crimson flock wallpaper were the ammonia fumes rising from a carpet that had long since offered neither cushioned comfort nor cheery decoration. Typed notes pinned above an open guestbook barked strict instructions regarding signing in and out, and a line in bold *and* capitals reminded visitors to ensure the front door remained closed at all times. I shook a tip box labelled 'For Your Friendly Staff' and took note of the hollow rattle.

'Oi, you're not nicking our tips, are you?' The nurse who had let us in seemed to be only half-joking.

We followed her up the fast lane of the staircase. The slow lane was for stair-chairs only.

'This is an example of a room, but they're all different. This is one of the bigger ones.'

I squeezed past David to get a better look and was alarmed to see a wispy-haired lady staring back at us intruders. 'Have I got visitors?' she asked, eyes wide with anticipation.

'Not today, Ellie. Just showing these nice men round,' shouted the nurse.

'Oh,' said Ellie, disappointed.

I smiled as compassionately as I could.

'I've got me own teeth,' ventured Ellie, as though ownership of her dentures was the deciding factor as to whether we'd stay or leave. 'See!' She tapped a finger on what were clearly false teeth.

'Nice,' said David.

She beckoned him closer so that she could whisper in his ear. 'Want to hold them? They won't bite!'

David declined, politely but firmly.

The glassed-in lounge area added nothing to the appeal of the place. Residents sat on hard-backed chairs lined against every wall. Some slept, others slurped noisily on drinks. Four floral so-fas faced each other across a coffee table in the centre of the room. Pensioners in various stages of dress and seemingly mental competence slouched over teacups. Some smiled as we entered, some said hello, and some continued staring at the carpet.

'It's bingo in ten minutes, so they're getting excited,' said the nurse as she handed us steaming cups with saucers. 'Excited' was not the word I'd have used, but presumably she knew her residents better.

David and I sat in silence for five minutes while we were examined by the more astute residents.

'Bit young for this, aren't you?' said a well-dressed lady from one of the sofas.

I laughed politely. 'We're checking it out for our nan. What do you reckon?'

The lady looked around and shrugged. 'It's no five-star hotel, but it's somewhere warm while you wait your turn.'

'Have you no family?' asked David.

'Plenty,' she said. 'But they've got their own lives to live. I'll make do here.'

As I gazed out at the frosty fields on the drive home, I thought how sad it must be to have lived a full and meaningful life only to have to 'make do' in your final years. Or months. Or even weeks. Nan deserved to go out with a bang, not idle her days away watching the rain and being bossed about with a bunch of others that had been dispatched to God's waiting room. I decided that after I'd flown back the next day I'd look into retirement homes in Tenerife.

CHAPTER FIVE

Back in the warmth of Tenerife, we had become 'nodding' friends with Alison and Stuart over the low white wall that separated our two small squares of ocean-facing garden in the El Beril complex.

Like many others, this friendly, fresh-faced couple had moved from the UK to Tenerife to start anew in sunnier climes, believing that the mere act of geographical relocation would provide a more thrilling life. Like those same many, they soon realised that even if the grass was greener, it still needed mowing, and nor was it entirely trouble-free: the pleasant patches were under continual siege from weeds and creepy crawlies and were also subject to periods of drought.

Some people contend that it's these very antagonists that keep life interesting, that without the weeds and the biting insects you can't appreciate the nice things in life. These are usually the same people who come out with such nonsense as 'no pain, no gain' and 'hard work never did anybody any harm'. Tell that to the millions who die of stress-related diseases every year.

Joy, my brother David and I had worked our fingers to the bone to make the Smugglers a success, and, like us, Alison and Stuart also weren't afraid to put in the hours. Alison walked dogs, worked in a bar in Playa de las Américas and hand-crafted greetings cards which she sold on a market stall in Los Cristianos. Stuart rented out sound equipment by day and pulled pints of beer at night.

None of these jobs were very stimulating, but Alison and Stuart put up with them in the hope that 'something else' would come along, the one big stroke of luck that would provide validation and significance, be it fame, infamy or an unexpected fortune. Something that would prove that life didn't have to be a succession of struggles.

Alison had been applying to every TV show that was relevant to her status as an expat in the sun. Finally, it seemed that one of the seeds she had planted would bear fruit. Over one early-morning nodding exchange, she enthused about a phone call she'd just received. '*Changing Rooms* have just been on,' she shouted giddily from across the wall. 'We're on a shortlist for their overseas special!'

I nodded, mid-yawn, trying to bring the ocean into focus through sleep-weary eyes. 'Excellent. That's… excellent.' Joy and I had become accustomed to Alison's cycle of moods. They spiralled from initial excitement over her latest attempt at fast fame, to despair as her dreams faded alongside a phone that refused to ring.

Changing Rooms was a popular British TV show fronted by the ever-beaming 'girl-next-door' Carol Smillie. The simple for-mat revolved around restyling one room in a house whose owner had either tired of the decor or, like Alison and Stuart, clamoured for TV attention. The homeowners would gush enthusiastically to the *Changing Rooms* team about what they would like to do with the room given the resources. On camera they also talked about hobbies, interests and any furnishing styles that they absolutely hated. They were then packed off for twenty-four hours while the team worked on the room. The facial expressions of the returning homeowners acted as a barometer as to whether the revamped room was a hit or a disaster. Most of the time there were tears of joy. Occasionally there would be genuine anger. Especially when the *Changing Rooms* team had purposefully chosen a pet hate and restyled the room accordingly just to elicit an extreme reaction.

'They'll let me know either way later this week,' continued Alison. She shot back inside her apartment, leaving me nodding at the ocean with an appropriate expression of feigned excitement.

Alison was no different to most of us treading water in our lives. She was desperate for someone to throw her a curveball, something that would sweep her out of her humdrum existence and into that fantasy world inhabited by the chosen few. Magazines, newspapers and TV shows offered glimpses into lives less ordinary, lives with celebrity trappings, lives that inspired public envy and private elation. While many were resigned to watching from afar, Alison saw no reason why she couldn't be part of it. Neither did I.

Maybe we'd had similarly encouraging upbringings. Maybe

we'd both seen through the artificial barriers that divided the populace into 'them' and 'us'. Maybe we both understood that the celebrated and famous were, on the whole, just people like us who'd had that lucky break. We knew that luck most often befell those who put themselves in positions where, if opportunity was to rain down from a silver-lined cloud, they'd be the ones standing directly underneath with a large bucket.

My own dreams were a little hazy. I wanted to be well known, admired, even, but not famous for the sake of it. I wanted to prove to myself that I was just as good and worthy as those I read about and watched in the media. In part, I guess I wanted to prove my own theory that in the developed world we are all born equal and life is what you make of it. Sure, there are those born into less advantaged backgrounds, but for the sake of simplicity I'm assuming a level playing field.

If Joy and I hadn't recklessly swapped a career in entrails and giblets on Bolton fish market for life as British bar owners abroad, we would never have become the 'local celebrities' of El Beril. And as small a sea as that may be, for seven years we were still considered big fish in that one holiday complex.

The difference now was that Alison was still active in her pursuit of a lucky break, and I wasn't. If just one of her optimistic applications came off, she would be privileged with a sneak peek behind the curtains of fame, even if it was only for a fleeting moment.

Two days later and that curtain started twitching as she got a thumbs-up from *Changing Rooms*. Unfortunately, Alison would soon come to realise that being in front of the cameras was not all it was cracked up to be.

In exceptional cases, *Changing Rooms* would spend a small fortune on converting a plain shoebox of a room into a child's fantasy world; for the most part, however, production costs on the programme were kept to a minimum. Never more so than when the entire crew and cast had to be shipped overseas. The producer had asked Alison over the phone if she could find locals to fill various menial roles at low cost, which is how I became Miss Smillie's chauffeur for the four-day shoot.

It struck me after my first couple of days with Carol, collecting her from the hotel in Playa de las Américas at seven thirty in the morning and dropping her back there at seven at night, that Carol was very much like Joy had been before life at the Smugglers Tavern took its toll. We were on first-name terms now of course – well, I was; Carol kept forgetting my name, but in her defence, she probably had a lot on her mind.

Both Carol and Joy took a genuine interest in every new person they met, bright eyes widening further with every minute detail extracted from whoever they were talking to. Both radiated an energy that was almost palpable, boosting those around them with instant feelgood like a nuclear battery charger. It was this quality that had endeared Joy to the customers in the bar, many of whom believed they'd found a new best friend in her. Although Joy naturally saw everybody as a potential friend, her warmth and conviviality eventually became her downfall. The sheer quantity of 'best friends' demanding her attention was exhausting, especially while running a business that afforded no time for real relationships. Ours included.

Both women were also very pretty, with shining, wondrous eyes, wide-open smiles that held nothing back, and understated curves that whispered suggestively rather than screamed for attention.

By the time I dropped her off at the airport with a parting kiss, I don't mind admitting I had become a little smitten with Smillie. She handed me a bottle of wine with words of gratitude for 'going the extra mile'. The wine became a prized possession and would never be consumed. I still have it now.

While I basked in the sunshine of the presenter's appreciation, two doors away, Alison and Stuart were less enamoured with their Carol Smillie experience. The conversion of the kitchen/living room in their El Beril apartment had left Alison in tears – bad for them, great for TV.

In their individual pre-makeover interviews, Alison had been adamant that she didn't want anything too modern or 'out there'. The bleep machine went into overdrive when the TV team's efforts at a 'spaceship interior' were revealed. While Stuart feigned approval, Alison told them in no uncertain words where they could stick the tinfoil effect on the coffee table, and in what orifice they could put the garish purple and silver sticky tape that striped their walls.

What made it worse was that the crew only had time to complete the refurb on those parts of the room that the camera would see. The NASA-meets-Poundstretcher effect stopped abruptly halfway down the walls of the kitchen area. The remaining three feet of off-white walls and honey-coloured pine door panels were concealed from a million eyes but not from the eyes of the two people who had to live with it.

It was half a job, and half a job done cheaply, and the day after the TV crew left, Joy, Alison, Stuart and I removed the stapling and sticky tape that held their fifteen minutes of fame together and tried to return the room to its original state. But the damage had been done. According to Alison, she felt her home had been violated beyond repair.

Later that month, we helped them relocate to a semi-dilapidated house in Tejina de Isora, a hillside village near the west coast, twenty minutes' drive from Playa de las Américas.

'It needs a bit of work,' said Alison as we placed cardboard boxes and black bin liners on the dusty white-tiled floor.

Joy and I surveyed the mess. If restoring their El Beril apartment to its pre-*Changing Rooms* state had proved too much work, I couldn't imagine the toil they faced to turn this half-house into a cosy home.

The space and isolation were the key factors for Alison and Stuart though, or more precisely for their two Alsatians. To me, it seemed like moving to another country. In El Beril we had a supermarket, a choice of restaurants, a beach, a communal swimming pool, tennis courts, street lighting and immaculate tarmac roads. Up there in Tejina, they had cacti, dust and a twenty-minute walk to civilisation. It felt dirty, lonely and a step back in time.

When we returned to El Beril that evening, I was glad to get back to the modern comforts of polished marble, straight walls, and windows and doors that didn't resist being opened and closed. Joy, however, had a different take on it, perhaps because she was still the (unwanted) centre of attention from ex-customers.

'I'm jealous,' she announced when we landed at El Beril.

'Of what?' I asked. 'Mould, mess and isolation?'

'Of the views, the peace, the privacy.'

'You'd move to somewhere like that?' My tone had risen a few octaves.

'I'd certainly think about it. Wouldn't you?'

'Erm, no thanks. I'm quite happy here.'

But as soon as I'd said it, doubts arose. A change of scenery! Something to shake us from this lethargy! Maybe it wasn't such a bad idea. Trouble was, I was too apathetic to do anything about it. We'd moved apartments five times during our bar days. Moving was hard work. And so was house-hunting. The opportunity would have to come to me.

CHAPTER SIX

First, though, I was on a mission to house-hunt for someone else, namely Nan, who had now been 'detained' in hospital for two weeks on doctor's orders. It was either keep her in hospital or have her transferred to the nearest available nursing home, which was over forty miles from her house, and, more inconveniently, from David's house in Clitheroe.

The doctor had insisted that it wasn't safe to have her live on her own given that she was so unsteady on her feet. She was also plagued with a cluster of infections and medical complaints that refused to budge even in the face of heavy-duty remedies or her own steely denial that there was 'owt' wrong.

Investigations revealed that the sunshine isles weren't exactly overrun with sunshine retirement homes, which came as something of a surprise. A good dose of Tenerife warmth had been prescribed to the UK's ill and afflicted since the late nineteenth century. In fact, it was this medical tourism that eventually opened the floodgates of Canary Island holidays for north Europeans with less wholesome desires.

Whereas in the last decades of the 1800s people came to Tenerife to improve their health, ironically, since the mid-1980s, the quality of a fortnight abroad has often been judged by how ill you've been able to get, a phenomenon not exclusive to Tenerife but one still extolled in last-night outings and post-holiday tales back home. The conversations invariably go something like this:

'Going home tomorrow.' Said with a glum face over a pint of lager and a whisky shot.

'How's it been?'

'Brilliant! Been rough as a badger's arse every morning.'

'Fantastic.'

'Thrown up three times in a week!'

'Doesn't get much better than that, does it?'

'S'been magic. Well... the bits I remember, anyway.'

'Good to hear. 'Nother pint and chaser?'

'Is the Pope Catholic?'

With such a switch in holidaymakers' aspirations, it should have come as no surprise that on Tenerife there was a lot more effort focused on making people ill than making people better.

There were plenty of hotels that drew the older crowd for a fortnight or slightly longer, and lots of self-catering apartments that Tenerife's 'swallows' reserved for the winter months years in advance. What there wasn't was a choice of residential complexes specifically geared to the expat silver set with on-site carers and bingo on-demand – a sure gap in the market, if any entrepreneurial readers are looking for a Tenerife niche. There was one, however. And it needed checking out.

Housed in a *finca* (farmhouse) in the western hills of the island, the cluster of single-storied buildings that made up this care home looked like an unfinished construction project from the outside. It wasn't much different inside.

In the nursing home David and I had visited in Clitheroe, typed notes and door locks ensured no illegal entries – or exits. Here, every corridor and doorway had waist-level childproof gates. It was like Alcatraz for the height-impaired.

From the reception area – a drab waiting room with exposed breeze-block walls – I was escorted down a steep stone staircase. Small bungalows the size of single-car garages surrounded an empty swimming pool that was awash with algae. Weeds sprouted from cracked floor tiles, and bits of broken furniture were piled in one corner. I expected an apology for the state of the place, or at least an explanation, but none was forthcoming, and the receptionist continued the tour seemingly blind to the decrepitude.

On a raised terrace overlooking the drained pool, four residents sat in the sun on plastic chairs, penned in on plastic grass that curled up at the edges like Aladdin's slippers. There was no shade and even though it was winter, the subtropical rays were still formidable. As we continued through the garden, it began to feel familiar. I was sure I'd seen the central pool when it was swimmable, not sprouting weeds, and at the back of my mind I knew I had sat in the communal lounge area, though probably not in such shabby seats.

Then I remembered – the nursing home used to be a restaurant and we'd eaten there at least twice. The dining area had hardly changed at all. Exposed stonework had threatened diners' legs even back then and was no less of a hazard today. The coarse stone could easily slice through the tissue-thin skin of calves and thighs if senior diners slipped off the cushions protecting them from the raw edges.

I also remembered that Nan had dined there with us one night, and that even then access to the bathrooms was far from easy for someone with mobility problems. Everything seemed to have been built on different levels, and you couldn't walk more than a few paces before your progress was halted by yet another set of stone steps.

If there was ever a place wholly unsuitable for use as a nursing home, it was this former restaurant in the hills. Yes, residents had no chance of fleeing without first navigating several flights of stairs, but they also had no chance of moving around the place without risking a serious stumble down lethal stone steps. It was a definite no-go. Back to the drawing board.

CHAPTER SEVEN

As Tenerife ambled towards twenty-first-century tourism, in March 2000 my wish to break free of our jingoistic surroundings was granted as, ironically, Joy and I took a step back into the previous century.

Two months after moving from El Beril into the hills of Tejina de Isora, Stuart had decided that he no longer cared for rural life, or indeed for Alison. He moved back to 'civilisation', sharing an apartment with a mate amidst the bars and clubs of Playa de las Américas, leaving Alison alone in the village with the two dogs.

Unable to drive, Alison was restricted to travelling by moped. With two large Alsatians in tow, this was no easy task. It wasn't long before the isolation became a burden. When the dark of night closed in on Tejina, she found restful sleep hard to come by as she lay in bed listening to the scuttling of lizards and the creaking of haphazardly built walls. Desperate to move back to a less lonely and more accessible location, she asked if we knew of any apartments available to rent in El Beril. Joy's eyes lit up.

Our complex, El Beril, had served a purpose and served it well. When we had the bar, we were only 178 paces from home (188 for Joy, who has shorter legs), which was just about all we could muster at the end of a busy night. The apartment was small, therefore easy to maintain with barely more than a flick of a duster and a couple of mop swishes in each direction. The complex was pretty, too, with its sprays of violet bougainvillea against whitewashed walls, and it allowed easy access to the treasures that life in a hot climate requires – a beach and a choice of watering holes.

To most people El Beril was, and still is, a pleasant place to spend your holidays. But being a resident in one of its 120 adjoining bungalows and two-storey apartments was like living in a goldfish bowl. Joy and I couldn't go anywhere without other El Berilians craning over the crisscrossed wooden beams of their balcony terraces to inquire where we were headed, where we'd been and what we'd had for lunch that day.

This problem wasn't exclusive to ventures beyond our front door. Our garden fence bordered a footpath that circumnavigated the complex. As we lay in the sunshine, minding our business, at least once an hour somebody would shatter the calm with inane conversation, interrupting Joy's afternoon doze. She would have to scramble to cover up from topless sunbathing while the strollers quipped how it was 'alright for some', or 'you've got a good life'. Or, worse still, 'you don't need to cover up for me, love' from a worryingly regular 'passer-by'. A small bulge in his fading speedos raised suspicions that he had been leaning on our fence longer than we deemed appropriate.

So, when Joy suggested a house swap whereby Alison would come back to live in El Beril and we would escape to the hills of Tejina, we were packed up and moved within the week. Naturally, this put an end to any plans we had of shipping Nan over from the UK to spend her final years with us. Her increasing ability to fall over even the tiniest of obstacles would be a challenge too far in a half-finished house on an uneven patch of Tenerife hillside.

The house in Tejina was on the edge of a *barranco* (ravine), one of hundreds of vertiginous drops that carve the island into slices of crusty pie. The building itself looked distinctly like it was still a work-in-progress. The two-storey cube had one too few coats of pale yellow paint over a rendered, whitewashed base. In places, the rendering had broken off, leaving patches of grey breeze-block. It looked like a decaying molar. But its location was its glory.

Perched alone above the unassuming agricultural village of Tejina de Isora, there were no impediments to a 180-degree view of the Atlantic some four miles away. Nature had done a fine job of turning what at first seemed like a lifeless plateau into a gorgeous meadow of ethereal beauty. Giant fingers of cacti swelled from clusters of euphorbia on either side of the *barranco*, while orange and black butterflies hovered above clumps of broom and lavender that freckled the surrounding plain with yellow and purple. Apart from a handful of detached properties stretching up the hill behind us, the only evidence of human intervention were the six long lines of cabbages, tomatoes and other less recognisable crops the landlord tended below the concrete patio that skirted the house on two sides.

As we placed the first of our cardboard boxes inside, it was evident that the troubles between Alison and Stuart had set in early. They clearly hadn't properly settled in, and the place still looked a lot like a storeroom. In a small box room off the living area, black irrigation tubing coiled around errant breeze-blocks like a plague of snakes. A solitary lightbulb dangled from a long cable poking through the plasterboard ceiling. In the far corner, a high stone step led to a doll's-house door. Through this lay another long, dark room that stretched almost the full length of the house. Inside, bales of straw and bags of chicken feed were piled on a raw concrete floor. An eyebrow-height ceiling added an *Alice in Wonderland* surrealism.

The kitchen, two bedrooms and white-tiled bathroom housed the cheapest of cheap mismatching fixtures and fittings. Wardrobes leant at jaunty angles, bed frames wobbled precariously, and personal injury threatened at every turn. Wooden kitchen chairs nipped at cheeks, plug sockets leapt from the walls, oversized bows of exposed electrical wires dangled from the ceiling, and razor-sharp aluminium window frames could only be closed with the persuasion of a mallet.

Upstairs was a separate apartment with its own entrance. We knew it was occupied, but its occupants remained a mystery. Alison had heard movement above but never actually seen who lived there. According to her, a car was occasionally parked halfway down the 150 feet of broken concrete that constituted a driveway at the side of the house. All we saw was the occasional twitching of a net curtain as we paraded back and forth along the garden path with boxes of books, crockery and knick-knacks.

A big concern with our move to Tejina was Fugly. Cats are wont to try and relocate to their original home, so to prevent this we had to lock her inside the house for the first week while we cleaned, arranged our furniture and bedded in.

While Joy scoured the white floor tiles and degreased the pine dining table in the kitchen, I set about refitting the light switches and electrical sockets that had popped from the wall. The faint whiff of burning as I did so triggered memories from the early days of Smugglers when I was electrocuted after running cables from a nearby house. A phantom tingle ran through my right arm again.

Grubby floral curtains concealed kitchen cupboards which were just cobweb-ridden spaces underneath the sink and granite worktop. We evicted the half-empty bottles of cleaning fluids, buckets, bricks and bugs that had made their home there and repopulated the spaces with our pans and crockery.

In the living room, our L-shaped sofa was positioned to afford views of the TV *and* the *barranco* through the sliding patio doors. It was the only place where the sofa would fit without creating an obstacle course, but it also forced those who sat on it to stare at a trio of worryingly large cracks in the wall behind the pine TV cabinet and shelves. Those with more structural engineering experience would have applied their skills to either remedy the situation or get the hell out. We decided on a more pragmatic route – out of sight, out of mind. Indoor plants of varying heights were bought and positioned to mask the danger.

And all the while, Fugly whined. She was not a happy cat. The unknown traumas that had plagued her tiny mind to date seemed to triple amidst the carnage of change, and her depression plummeted to the point where she wailed like a banshee day and night. Normal cats could be placated with love and attention. Her mood would only be lifted by sinking her teeth and claws into whatever she could reach.

Unsurprisingly, Fugly's venomous nature won us no favours from Rigsby, the nickname we had assigned to our new landlord due to his uncanny likeness to the dour property owner in the 1970s British sitcom *Rising Damp*. Rigsby was not only the landlord of our house, he was also its builder. I suspected that the construction had been something of a suck-it-and-see challenge, the kind you take on after a few too many beers with a mischievous crowd: 'I bet you can't build a house out of wheelbarrows and birds' nests.'

To be fair, at first sight, and ignoring the diarrhoea-coloured paint, it looked like a proper house with all the right assets in the right places – namely walls, floors and a roof. It was only through closer examination that its flaws were exposed.

The same applied to Rigsby himself. He had the appearance and manner of a friendly uncle, eager to please and with a warm smile. But on the second or third encounter, I began to notice his physical quirks.

It was evident that he wore a black hairpiece. It was also evident that any labelling indicating front and back must have worn off. Some days he would arrive with a neat synthetic side-parting high on his forehead and a tuft of black fanning over his collar at the back; on other occasions, the side-parting would be at the back of his head and the tuft would fan out above his eyebrows like a startled scarecrow. Many a morning the tuft would hover over one of his ears. Its positioning was as unpredictable as his infrequent visits.

We estimated Rigsby's age at somewhere in the upper forties, low fifties range, which meant that presumably he still worked. The low rent he received from us, and any profit from the produce grown in the *barranco* would surely not be enough to support a family. It later emerged that he owned a succession of self-built rental homes throughout the municipality, which in Tenerife terms put him in the bracket of property baron.

The contract we signed was certainly not amateur, either – thirty pages of legalese including an inventory of every item in the property from teaspoons to bedheads, plus a list of rental conditions that covered everything from prompt monthly payments and party restrictions, to flea infestations and animal prohibitions.

Fortunately, his anti-pet stance had been softened when he'd reluctantly agreed to Alison moving in with her two dogs a few months earlier. When we showed him our seemingly innocuous white bundle of fluff (from a safe distance, of course), he voiced no objections. On his second visit to see how we were getting on, however, he witnessed the bundle of fluff's true colours. Standing on her hind legs, she tore towards him like a shrunken, rabid polar bear.

'*Qué está? Qué está?*' (What is it? What is it?) he asked, pointing, mouth open in surprise as he hastily backed down the garden path.

CHAPTER EIGHT

Two weeks after Fugly's introduction to Rigsby, Joy and I were sipping a musty local wine on our terrace as the sun sank behind the silhouette of La Gomera, Tenerife's nearest neighbouring island. 'Why are we throwing a party?' I asked.

'To celebrate. A moving-in do to show people where we live. I'm proud of this place, aren't you?'

I looked at the mustard-coloured cube of breeze-blocks blighting what was otherwise a pretty pastoral landscape. 'I'm proud of the views.'

'There you go,' said Joy. 'We can show off the views.'

I peered around her elbow as she began to scribble down names.

We had intended to have only a small party, make it low-key. But as so often happens with events like these, things got quickly out of hand.

First there was the guest list. 'Just our closest friends,' I suggested as Joy sat, pen poised over paper.

The pen hung in the air for a few uncomfortable seconds.

'We haven't really got any close friends,' admitted Joy.

We pondered this for a while. It was true. We had become social hermits, content in our rural isolation. 'Well that's good. This patio won't hold that many anyway,' I said, trying to find a positive. The low-walled garden couldn't accommodate more than about thirty people. There was also a two-inch-wide crack along the length of the paving at the side of the house. The weight of too many people could conceivably cause it to break off and go flying into Rigsby's neat furrows at the edge of the scrubland.

Not having any real friends was a common moan in Tenerife, as in any place with a large and transient expat population. Despite this, our guest list grew, in direct proportion to the wine consumed that day. And so did our aspirations.

One person who wouldn't be coming to the party was Nan. Yet another fall had put her back in hospital for a week. With the reluctance you'd expect from someone who'd enjoyed adult independence for over seven decades, she'd eventually agreed that continuing to live in her two-up two-down terraced house in Clitheroe was no longer viable, and David had found her 'the best room in the best nursing home' in the Ribble Valley. Nan needed twenty-four-hour care and deserved to have someone looking after her, even if it meant sacrificing self-sufficiency.

By the time two empty bottles of Viña Sol lay on the black cinders, we'd decided on Smugglers-themed food, including the return of our ever popular Hawaiian burgers, and we were tottering around the garden trying to find the best place to put a live band.

If hangovers serve any purpose, it's to bring you back down to earth the morning after. Which is why our lofty ambitions were thankfully scaled down over morning coffee.

The weather gods were in a particularly jolly mood on the day of the party. Wisps of white cloud came and went like curious neighbours watching the transformation of our cement and volcanic-gravel garden into a colourful jamboree of fluttering banners, balloons and tablecloths.

Overcoming our reluctance to get reacquainted with patrons from our Smugglers days, we had decided to combine the housewarming party with a Smugglers reunion. We were still receiving so many invites to meet up again that we figured rather than endure individual evenings, we could bring everyone together in one big social event. Besides, we needed to get the numbers up to a reasonable, though not dangerous, level. We didn't want to look like we had no friends, after all.

Frank, the dour truck driver from Oldham was the first to arrive. Like most of the old faces, we hadn't seen him since the bar days. Unlike most, he hadn't kept in touch, but Joy and I were both curious about what he was up to. Maybe he had finally overcome the obstacles that had been thrown in his way, including inadvertently marrying a lesbian and having an alcoholic as a flatmate. Perhaps he was living life to the full now he had unburdened himself of both.

He wasn't. 'Why the hell would you want to live in a dump like this?' He sauntered into our garden, hands in pockets, shoulders rounded as if weighted with chains.

'Good to see you again, Frank,' said Joy cheerfully. She gave him a peck on each cheek.

He grunted.

I held out a hand. 'Frank! Long time!'

He turned back to Joy. 'Still with that useless twat then.' He gave a wry smile. 'Didn't bring a bottle or anything. Thought you'd probably still have plenty from the bar. Do I have to get myself a beer or what?'

I watched through the kitchen window as the patio started to fill with faces from our other life. Joy had already slipped into hostess mode, greeting the ex-patrons like long-lost friends with earnest warmth and what looked to me like genuine smiles. She was a formidable actress alright! Or maybe it was genuine, and I was just a miserable, unsociable git. I decided it was probably a combination of both as I carried two jugs of sangria into the fray.

'Hello,' said a low voice over my shoulder. A bespectacled man with a wispy comb-over, sagging shoulders and downbeat eyes smiled nervously. It was Roger, the ex-community president of El Beril. At least I'd heard he was 'ex'. The rumours were that he'd been kicked out of the role by a young, dynamic German bungalow owner who'd been lobbying the complex owners non-stop for months. But out of the corner of my eye I saw what looked like a clipboard. Surely he hadn't come to our party with a checklist?

'For you,' he said quietly, offering me the flat package. 'And Joy, of course. A little housewarming gift. Is that Smugglers sangria?' I poured him a glass. He held it aloft. 'To new beginnings.' For the rest of the party he stood alone, nursing his glass to his chest and nodding formally at the others, unable to join in.

Wayne, our bar odd-job man, had claimed a place on the gravel. He was sitting side-by-side with a man I didn't recognise. Their plastic chairs were turned away from the gathering crowd and they stared over the *barranco* as if watching a game of cricket.

Wayne was still the same: scruffy, near-black hair tied back in a ponytail, and a black Rolling Stones vest revealing inked ladies and sharp-toothed tigers. 'Want some?' he hissed as he sucked in aromatic smoke through clenched teeth.

'No thanks, mate. How you keeping?'

'Oh, you know, up and down, bit of this, bit of that. Nice place you got here, mucker.'

'Thanks. Needs a bit of work.'

'You know where to come.'

I smiled at the man sitting next to him, waiting for an introduction. The man stood and shook my hand, firmly.

'John.' There was a faint accent – Dutch, German perhaps. He stood tall, with a calm confidence. 'I hope you don't mind me coming?'

'No, not at all. More the merrier and all that.' Who the hell was he? 'I feel like I know you, but—' I felt a tap on the shoulder.

'Joe! How damned decent of you to invite us.' It was Michael and his shy wife, Sheila, both in their sixties. Our distant 'neighbours'.

We had invited them partly to break the ice and partly to make sure they wouldn't call the police if the noise kept their goats awake or whatever. Joy and I had progressed from polite nodding as our car passed theirs to waving across the *barranco* when one or both of us were hanging washing out to dry.

Michael wore a permanent grin and a neatly pressed pink shirt. This, along with his loud, confident tone, suggested financial success, a suspicion backed up by the bottle of vintage red that he presented to me with pride. 'Châteauneuf-du-Pape,' he announced, pushing it into my chest. 'Save it for yourselves.' He leant in. 'It's not for these riffraff.'

'Thanks,' I said, and dangled a half-empty jug in front of him. 'Sangria?'

'Erm, no thanks. Champagne? Cava?'

'We'll have two glasses of sangria, won't we, Michael.' Sheila smiled apologetically. 'He can be *such* a snob.'

We had also tried to invite the people living upstairs, having knocked on three separate occasions. Each time we heard a shuffle of feet on the other side of the door, but they were always scuttling in the opposite direction.

Over Sheila's head I spied the net curtains in the second-floor apartment twitch again. A stern lady pulled on the shoulders of a wide-eyed toddler, drawing her away from the window. I smiled up, hoping for a reaction, but the child's face remained expressionless as she disappeared behind the shabby lace.

I tried to work my way back to the stranger across the garden, but Joy intervened. 'I think you need to check on somebody,' she said, worried.

'Who, the guy in the corner with Wayne?'

'No. Our little girl. I thought she was locked in our bedroom, but the door's open. I think somebody has let her out.'

Damn. If there was one thing that could spoil the party, it would be an escaped psychotic cat. However, she was nowhere to be seen.

'JOE?'

I instinctively ducked and turned to see Justin beaming at me from the doorway. At the Smugglers, this lanky pre-teen had a habit of magically appearing from nowhere, and his teleportation skills were obviously still intact. His thought processes were completely different to us humans too. In fact, it was entirely possible that he was an alien.

We first realised this at the bar with the daily bursts of illogic that he spouted while trailing after us as we mopped or restocked. 'So,' he would always begin, 'if Buster [our bar cat] thinks he's a dog, what does he see when he looks in the mirror?' Or 'Why do people wear trunks when they swim in the sea but not when they go out in the rain?'

'Justin! Scared me to death. How you doing?'

'I'M ALRIGHT.' He pointed to his ear. 'I GOT A HEARING AID.'

'Ah, right. Is it switched on, only you're talking REALLY LOUD?'

'NO. I'M SAVING THE BATTERY.'

'For what?'

'IN CASE THERE'S AN EMERGENCY.'

I knew I probably shouldn't have asked, but I did anyway. 'Like what?'

'LIKE IF I WAS CROSSING THE ROAD AND SOMEBODY SHOUTED A CAR WAS GOING TO HIT ME. IF THERE WAS

NO CHARGE LEFT ON MY BATTERY, I'D BE DEAD.'

'But how will you know when to turn it on?'

'I JUST TOLD YOU.' Justin looked at me as if I was simple, but before I could point out the flaw in his logic, he shouted again, only louder. 'WHAT'S THAT?'

I turned towards the direction of his finger. As I did, a flash of white exploded from the top of the kitchen dresser, bounced off the side of my neck and skidded, cartoon-like, through the kitchen doorway into the garden.

I followed as the admiring 'Aahs' turned to pained 'Ows', and then to quiet screams.

On seeing so many people, Fugly had panicked, lashed out at anyone who'd dared to so much as look at her, and leapt over the garden wall. From there, with a concrete barrier between her and the burgeoning crowd, she hissed, snarled and generally was as menacing as she could manage.

Just as the panicked screams of our guests subsided, they rose again from around the wrought-iron chairs and tables in the middle of the garden. Heads swished away from Fugly and towards the melee as drinks were spilled, chairs vacated and children whisked off the black ash.

'They're biting – the lizards!' cried Justin's mum, now standing on one of the chairs.

We'd never experienced vicious lizards in Tenerife, but, sure enough, we watched as they darted out from under the rocks and nipped at bare toes. The biggest was a good eighteen inches from beak to tail, and where previously a swish of the foot or flick of the hand had sent them scarpering back to their crevices, today, no amount of shooing would dispatch the grey scaly brute or his gang members. It was a reptile revolution, and what a day to have picked!

The twenty or so people who'd been socialising in the ashy garden area rushed to the safety of solid concrete. Or at least they thought it was safe.

I could see there were too many people on the part of the paving that had a huge crack. 'Move back,' I urged, but too late.

Justin had put his full weight on the wall as he leant over to try and placate Fugly, who was still threatening to attack from the rear. Then he disappeared. Along with a six-foot section of wall.

'Justin!' screamed his mum.

'Fugly!' screamed Joy.

'Move back,' I yelled, just as another loud crack and a gravelly crunch caused the slab of concrete they were standing on to rise up and start moving towards the edge of the slope like a family-sized surfboard.

Michael, Sheila, Justin's mum, Frank and I jumped back as it too slid over the edge of our garden and into the *barranco*.

Through the dust I could see the white figure of Fugly weaving through the cacti and broom, ears and body low to the ground. What I couldn't see was Justin.

Joy held my arm as I stepped onto the remaining rubble and peered into the abyss, where a huge slab of concrete now covered the space into which Justin had fallen.

'Justin?'

There was no answer. I called again.

'YES,' shouted a voice in my ear.

I nearly fell down the slope. Justin was standing next to me, peering into the *barranco*. I peered at him, trying to work out his witchcraft.

'SEE, THAT'S THE KIND OF EMERGENCY I WAS TALKING ABOUT.'

Mercifully, no one had suffered anything more serious than a bruise or a scratch, along with the embarrassment of suddenly being the centre of attention.

The collapse of the wall acted like a show finale and our guests, figuring that nothing else could top that spectacle, began to drift away.

Wayne and his mystery guest were the last to leave. 'Want me to fix that?' Wayne said, staring at the gap in our wall.

I nodded.

'Tomorrow do you?'

I nodded again. They turned to leave.

'Sorry, John,' said Joy to the mystery man, 'you've got to tell me where I know you from.'

'Owns a chain of restaurants, don't you, mucker?' said Wayne. 'Giving me a lift back in that Porsche, top of your drive.'

The man flashed a toothpaste-ad smile at us. 'You really don't remember me, do you?'

We both shook our heads.

Still smiling, he took himself by his collar and walked towards the door.

'You can't be!' said Joy.

He winked. 'Johan. King of Tenerife once more.' He leant in. 'But now king of property development, not of a wigwam on Spaghetti Beach.'

In our early days at the bar, Johan had been one of the first challenging customers we'd had to deal with. A scruffy, surfer-haired hippy, he would frequent the Smugglers dressed in his idiosyncratic style, which nearly always married ripped jeans and items more commonly associated with rubbish bins. Not content with drawing attention through his appearance, he would also elicit wary glances by singing loud choruses from Broadway musicals.

Tolerating his eccentricity proved to be far easier and less energy-consuming than enforcing any exclusion zone. So we put up with his musicality, his insistence that he was the King of Tenerife, and his inability to pay for the occasional meals and drinks he consumed.

During a brief period of flu-induced sobriety, we learned from Johan that when he'd left university his father had handed him a bundle of cash and told him to make something of himself. A spaced-out nomad was probably not what his dad had in mind.

However, we always found him to be deeply intelligent, as well as happy and relatively harmless (read the first book to find out why only 'relatively'). In fact, when he eventually stopped coming to the bar, we assumed he was either dead or had straightened himself out and was following a path more in keeping with the one his dad had imagined.

That night, I lay in bed reliving the day. Some people, like Justin and Wayne, hadn't changed at all. Others had lost their way – Brian, for one, his spark and confidence snuffed out now that he'd lost his perfect role.

I thought of Johan's transformation, the way he had (literally) picked himself up by his collar and, from such a low launching pad, had hit great heights. It gave me hope.

CHAPTER NINE

Following brief but enjoyable careers in painting, and chauffeuring smiley celebrities, while hope stewed in the background, I secured another fill-in job with a friend who had started a marble-floor-polishing business. Marble tiles were the preferred floor covering in Tenerife for most households and this, plus the fact that there was little competition in the domestic field, ensured that the demand for Marbleman was phenomenal.

The polishing contraption comprised a motorbike grip attached to a motor that spun an eighteen-inch scouring pad at high speed. My brief training covered what chemicals to use and in what order to apply them so that the mirror-like sheen that had been blurred by high heels, furniture scratches or water stains could be restored. More importantly, my 'driving' instruction included how to tame the spinning beast so it didn't career into furniture or gouge huge spurs out of the marble. Upon graduation, me and my 600-rpm friend were dropped off by a dusty van at private apartments and villas and let loose on their floors.

The buffing involved shuffling methodically at a snail's pace from one corner of the room to the other, slowly sweeping the machine from side to side to a monotone hum. A living room in a small apartment would take at least two hours to cover. It was mind-numbing but well paid, and the glass-like finish provided immense satisfaction to both operator and apartment owner.

My employer also happened to be a bass guitar player and was in the throes of getting a band together. Which was convenient. Within weeks we had a rehearsal space in his garage-cum-storeroom, where we met two nights a week. Days were spent sheening floors while plugged into a Walkman learning the drum patterns of new songs.

Julian the singer was an old hand on the Tenerife circuit and through his contacts it was easy to try out a few short, unpaid gigs at small, family-run bars. Our set list expanded in direct relation to the hours spent marble polishing and before long we had a big enough repertoire to play a full two-set gig. Which was just as well, as we'd been asked to play a regular Saturday-night spot at a nightclub on Golf del Sur, an estate of apartments and hotels sandwiched between a twenty-seven-hole golf course and the ocean, fifteen minutes' drive from Playa de las Américas.

Being in a working band again was exhilarating. I hadn't played a kit on stage since I'd guest drummed for Steve's band, my friend-turned-foe who'd stabbed me in the back by having an affair with Joy during our bar career (see Book Two).

In the year 2000 there weren't many full live bands working the circuit. Bar owners were, quite understandably, keener to pay for one man and his backing tracks than cough up thrice that for three alcohol-fuelled musicians. Westlife and the Backstreet Boys were in the charts, and not everybody wanted live rock. But in the words of Neil Young, 'rock and roll can never die', and there was, as ever, a niche audience fully appreciative of purist musical entertainment.

Julian was still doing one-man gigs, but thanks to his contacts, our group, the Joneses, was soon offered a three-night headline slot vacated by the former house band at the Soul Cellar (now Papagayo), one of the biggest clubs on the Veronicas nightlife strip. It was open-air and a big hit with groups of young holidaymakers corralled there by tour operators. Pub crawls involving up to two hundred revellers would converge at midnight and turn the moonlit dance floor into a writhing serpent of sunburnt limbs and flailing hair.

Party night for the band was every Tuesday, Thursday and Saturday from 11pm until 2am. We were plied with drinks, pointed towards a stage shrouded in dry ice and pulsating with light effects, and presented to an audience already high on ecstasy, speed, alcohol and holiday spirit. Most of them were happy with no more than a vaguely recognisable wall of sound to dance to, but Julian was a stickler for perfection and despite our intake of Jack Daniel's, our reputation as the south's best band grew. And we were getting paid!

Another highlight for me was that I could dip into the manic, neon-frenzied environment we'd left behind and then return to our new normality in the hills. It felt like a mini holiday. At 11.30pm I would leave the silence of Tejina in a taxi, whizzing past the darkened houses and empty streets. Within twenty minutes I was in a world just coming to life. Alighting at the top end of Troya Beach, each step along the seafront took me closer to the hum and sparkle of downtown Las Américas, through the cacophony of competing bars and clubs and with the buzz of knowing I'd be on stage in an hour. By the time I hopped onto the stage to tighten the drum skins and adjust the mics, my mood could not have been any brighter.

It was always going to come to an end though. For Jim and me, playing in a band was a hobby. The fact that we got paid was a bonus. For Julian, however, it was a career. This was how he paid his bills. Days were spent learning new songs and perfecting backing tracks for his solo and duo acts, evenings were about taking those songs to the stage. He was good, of that there was no question, an accomplished guitarist, singer and song arranger, but he was also greedy. Our gigs did not end with our flurry of chord striking, cymbal crashing and flashing lights, and then our 'Thank you, you've been the best crowd ever.' No, Julian always had one final task: a visit to the club manager to try and squeeze more money out of him for the next gig. 'But look how many people we've brought in. If we weren't on, you wouldn't get half this crowd.'

He was cocky, but that wasn't unusual among the more successful acts in Tenerife, and in that circle, success on the island was measured by the fee commanded. Naturally, there was a limit to how much each bar or club owner was prepared to pay, and a limit to how long they would put up with Julian's incessant badgering for more. At the Soul Cellar, this point arrived quicker than any of us had anticipated. After two months

Julian announced that we wouldn't be playing at the Soul Cellar any more and that he would soon find us another gig.

The other gig never materialised. By the end of summer 2000, it was obvious that Tenerife as a low-cost tourist destination had passed its peak. TV programmes in the UK were focusing on the filth and depravity of the Veronicas strip, following groups of revellers as they drank, swore, shagged and vomited their way through a week of juvenile debauchery. The authorities decided that the island needed a new, more sustainable image.

They began with an iron-fisted clampdown on the scruffiest and noisiest nightlife venues. Where laws weren't being broken, new ones were implemented which put the bars and clubs on the wrong side of legality. The rug was being pulled from Tenerife's bread-and-butter tourism in ways that defied belief.

New rules, which might not seem outlandish these days but in the early 2000s were bank-balance breakers for many proprietors, included obligatory air-conditioning and emergency exits, no sandwich boards advertising entertainment or menus, no awnings that extended over the pavement, and no furniture on the pavement unless that space was owned by the bar.

In hindsight, these rules were quite reasonable, but until then the bars and clubs of Veronicas had operated without the need to comply with health and safety regulations. Many were 'protected' by organisations that had a foothold in both the underworld and the enforcement world. We had experienced this ourselves in our days as bar owners, both when uniformed police would walk in and happily be 'distracted' from our legal oversights if free beer was forthcoming, and from close encounters with local extortion gangs.

We saw the same thing play out in Veronicas, in a bar that was operated by a friend of the band's. It was here that we would debrief after a gig with a table full of Dorada beer and tequila shots. Gary, the bar owner, would sit drinking with us but all the time looking over his shoulder at the two entrances. Even to those with zero knowledge of planning regulations, his bar clearly was not a legal entity. Gary had 'bought' a corridor between two clubs, deep in the depths of a Veronicas basement. It was kitted out with an assortment of chairs, stools and benches, a small, walkaround bar the central focus.

The owner of the clubs to either side didn't mind this mini competition from Gary, mainly because the day after Gary bought it, he sold on both clubs to a Russian gangster, who we'll call Psycho, for two reasons – because he was, and because that's what everybody else in Veronicas called him.

Psycho's vision was to combine both clubs into one mega-club. Naturally, he wasn't too pleased that Gary's hallway obstructed his plans, and no amount of subsequent 'persuasion' could make Gary give it up. Gary was stubborn to the point of stupid. He'd owned the bar for three months, during which time he'd been threatened on an almost daily basis and been hospitalised four times, twice by the police. Still he wouldn't move.

'Why?' I often asked, after gigs.

It was always the same answer. 'Because it's *my* sodding bar. I've always wanted to have my own boozer. It's my dream come true.'

I would look around at the shabby makeshift hallway, empty as usual. I would see the bruising from Gary's latest battering fading into his drawn, anxious complexion, note his fingers drumming on the handle of the omnipresent baseball bat leaning against his chair. '*This* is your dream?' I'd ask.

And then one night we were met with the charred remains of his dream. And Gary was gone.

One May breakfast-time a few months after Gary's demise, a bulldozer driver sat waiting in his cab alongside the strip of late-night bars in Las Veronicas. As the last of the bemused club-goers emerged into the sunlight, shielding their dilated pupils like vampire zombies, the driver fired up the engine, sending tiny clouds of black into the big blue above. Police cars suddenly arrived, followed by men in hard hats who waved clipboards at the stragglers, shepherding them further away from the bars.

At 8.15am the bulldozer screamed as the driver released the brake. Its caterpillar tracks advanced, crunching the paving stones below as it ploughed through Veronicas' oceanfront bars, clubs, late-night supermarkets and even later-night strip joints. Glass shattered, white plastic chairs and tables popped, and the metal poles that had propped up colourful canvas awnings clattered to the ground in domino fashion.

It was a defining moment in Tenerife's tourism history. Like myself, the island was passing from reckless adolescence into adulthood. From then on, new licences were drawn up and ruthlessly enforced, covering everything from live entertainment to catering, safety regulations to advertising. Bars and clubs were faced with huge bills for complying with the necessary reforms, additional licence fees for putting on music of any kind, and massive fines for flouting any of the new laws, all of which resulted in the top DJs and the most expensive entertainers being laid off. In pursuit of the high fees they were used to, the DJs moved off Tenerife and on to emerging hotspots like Ayia Napa in Cyprus, San Antonio in Ibiza and the Black Sea resorts of the new kid on the block, Bulgaria. The reign of Playa de las Américas as Europe's number-one party destination had come to an end.

To fill the gap, an overseas promotional campaign was launched, its brief to tempt the UK market with 'the other side of Tenerife'. The tropical foliage of Tenerife's lush northern slopes flashed promises of green exotica on the rain-stained sides of London's double-decker buses. It was time for me to explore the other side, too.

CHAPTER TEN

Even though we'd moved out of the tourist enclave when we came to Tejina, that didn't mean we immediately became immersed in village life. The main problem, of course, was our lack of proficiency with the Spanish language. This severely limited our social, cultural and entertainment opportunities. Although we had picked up plenty of bar and restaurant Spanish, beyond that, we were stumped. And because of this, we weren't able to feel part of the local scene, which meant we knew very little about the real Tenerife.

We had adopted nothing of the Canarian lifestyle except drinking Dorada beer and succumbing to a daily siesta between the hours of two and four. It was hardly what you could call a cultural conversion.

It was time to integrate more. Until our move into the yonder, we had kept to our own, like many of the island's expats, enjoying our little England in the sun. We had lived in a holiday resort, mixed with other British people, watched *Coronation Street* and *EastEnders*, and continued to be drawn to the supermarket shelves stocked with HP Sauce, Custard Cream biscuits and Campbell's Chunky Soup.

The more I thought about it, the more ashamed I felt. To have lived in a foreign environment for almost nine years, cocooned inside a bubble of homeland patriotism, felt uncomfortable, arrogant, even. It was like gate-crashing a party, blanking the host and sitting in a corner refusing to join in any of the arranged fun and games. Perhaps it was an intrinsic part of the British psyche, a kind of colonialism in miniature – invade a place, ignore its cultural identity and pursue your own way of living.

Joy and I had begun having Spanish lessons at home once a week, but it was slow going. The countless verb endings and the concept of gendered nouns were difficult to grasp, but it was a start. And one that I hoped would enable me to solve the mystery of our reclusive upstairs neighbours.

Rigsby merely ignored my questions or pretended that he didn't understand whenever I quizzed him about them. So, armed with a smattering of new vocabulary and a Smugglers-style apple pie that Joy had baked, I knocked on their door again. I knew they were home. The car was parked outside, and with an ear cupped to the door, I could hear a television at whisper volume.

The first tentative knocks brought no response.

'*Tengo una tarta para ti*,' I pressed. (I have a cake for you.) I continued knocking.

After sixty seconds of continual rapping on the varnished door, it suddenly opened, just a couple of inches on a safety chain but enough to reveal a silver-haired lady dressed in ankle-length black. Her hair was tousled like she hadn't brushed it in weeks, and her skin was etched with deep lines that conveyed a sense of perpetual worry.

I heard a soft voice from behind her. '*Quién es?*' (Who is it?)

The silver-haired lady turned her head and hissed, '*Cállate!*' (Shut up!) She turned back and looked from my face to the pie and back again, waiting for an explanation.

I dug deep into the weeks of lessons with Miguel, our Spanish teacher. 'I'm a Joe, it's neighbour.' I smiled. 'That is a cake of apple for yours.' I extended my arm towards the gap in the door. Clearly the pie was not going to fit. The lady eyed it suspiciously. One of us had to concede. The door closed, and I heard the safety chain jangle.

The door reopened and the lady stepped outside, pulling it almost closed behind her. She took the apple pie and her mouth briefly curled into a twitch of appreciation. '*Gracias*,' she murmured, then slid back inside and shut the door.

I stared at the wood panel for a moment and listened to the chain being reinstated. It was a breakthrough, but I was still none the wiser. *Poco a poco*, I thought. Little by little.

But it was not to be. Several nights later, Joy and I lay in bed listening to the scraping of furniture on the floor above, and then they were gone.

Flushed with the semi-success of my conversation with our now ex-neighbour, I wanted to plug myself deeper into Canarian culture, but not just there in the village. I needed to venture out, to get to the heart of Tenerife. I wanted not just to see the real Tenerife but to feel it, be in it, experience it with Canarian eyes. There was only one thing for it – I would tour the island's less-visited towns and villages the local way, by bus.

Joy had no such yearning. 'Spend all day on a bus? I'd rather eat my own eyeball,' was her response to my invitation. I took that as a no.

I wanted to see if I could circumnavigate the whole island in a clockwise direction, covering all 213 miles of coastline, or as much of it as physically possible, using nothing but the unfortunately named TITSA public bus service. I'd take in the tourist areas of the south, the local black-sand seaside towns of the west, the high mountains of the interior, the timeless agricultural villages of the north, the hidden hamlets of the northeast, and the windy plains of the east. Surely with so many environments and different landscapes I would find the real Tenerife – real scenery, real Tenerifians, real life.

My plan was to get off wherever took my fancy, take random detours and get up close and personal with Canarians going about their daily lives away from the contrived commerciality of twenty-first-century tourism. I would speak nothing but Spanish, order only what the person next to me was eating and mimic the mannerisms of authentic islanders that I came across. In short, I would be Canarian for a day.

CHAPTER ELEVEN

My journey into Canarian integration started at Costa Adeje bus station, located inland, next to the cement-slab architecture of the Magma Convention Centre at the back end of Playa de las Américas. Why anybody would position a bus station in one of the least pedestrian-friendly places in Costa Adeje was beyond me, but this is just one of dozens of WTF(!) traffic marvels on the island, as those who have lived in Tenerife for any length of time will know very well. Others include pedestrian zones on roundabout exits, motorway signs that compel speeds of 120, 80 and 60 kilometres per hour all within the space of thirty yards, and pedestrian lights that are entirely out of sync with the potentially fatal ebb and flow of road traffic.

I scoured the station for the number 473 from Las Américas to Los Gigantes, which departed on the half hour throughout the day. While its Canarian passengers slouched unconcernedly on benches as they waited, a dozen or so Brits had already formed a neat line underneath the 473 sign. In light of my determination to become more Canarian, I flopped against a billboard and tried to act as disinterested as possible.

By 7.50 those in line were checking their watches and exchanging expressions of exasperation. The Canarians and I milled some more. Several minutes later the big green bus swung into place, verbally confirmed by each Brit in the queue, as though not acknowledging its arrival would have been impolite in some way.

'It's here now.'

'Here it is.'

'About bloody time!'

The foreigners clambered aboard bearing bus maps, walking sticks and bush hats. The locals waited patiently behind them, calmly resigned in the knowledge that foreigners always, without fail, insert their Bono cards into the ticket machine every which way but the right one.

The driver's muttering grew more agitated with each explanation. The foreigners stared at him with the kind of bewilderment seen on the faces of children when first introduced to algebra. I was determined not to do the same. Like every good Canarian, I resisted the urge to smile or thank the driver, even when he snatched my ticket and reinserted it in the machine the right way round. I blushed. A fall at the first hurdle!

Eventually we were up and running. Once the high-rise hotels and reams of bars had become mere flecks in the rear-view mirror, the 473 passed through a succession of black-sand seaside resorts on the west coast favoured by Canarian beachgoers, including Playa San Juan, Alcalá and Playa de la Arena.

Los Gigantes also had a pleasant little beach that made a

peaceful spot for a lethargic afternoon. Though it would have been even more peaceful if it wasn't situated at the foot of a sheer 300-foot cliff that occasionally let loose a shower of rocks and dust on unsuspecting beachgoers.

For me, this north-western town merely served as a transit point for my next leg. As I stepped off the 473 and onto the 325 destined for Puerto de la Cruz on the north coast, I was feeling quite pleased with myself. I'd managed not to do the British thing and acknowledge the driver with a cheery 'Thank you' as I got off.

The 325 wound its way inland and up into the mountains, past clusters of wild cacti, their prickly fruit throbbing red at the side of the road like hitchhikers with sore thumbs. Soon, the on-board chatter subsided as I, like the other novice TITSA travellers, realised that scenic though these mountain roads were, they weren't wide enough to accommodate two large vehicles side-by-side. There was a communal intake of breath every five minutes as our bus driver miraculously slotted the number 325 between an oncoming lorry and the alarming precipice beneath us.

Twenty minutes later and the landscape had changed again. Solitary pine trees poked above yellow broom as we entered the mountain town of Santiago del Teide. The bus pulled over beside a tiny white church midway along the tree-lined main street. Several people in tight Gore-Tex T-shirts and trousers alighted, presumably to swap to the 355, which would take them over the peak to our left, then corkscrew down to Masca, Tenerife's Shangri-La, a remote and traditional village that clings to the slopes and from where a three-hour walk to the ocean beckons the hardiest.

With the bus stationary, two old boys shuffled to the front and joined the driver on the pavement. All three sucked furiously on self-rolled cigarettes before flicking the butts into the road and getting back on.

I guess we would have moved off straight away had their conversation come to an end. But it hadn't. The remaining passengers stared at the duo as they continued to talk and cackle with the seated driver for a further five minutes.

The bus creaked and groaned as it climbed for another twenty minutes. The driver seemed to be having a personal battle with it now as it lurched with every gear change, the clutch squealing like a pig in a panic. Somehow he got it to crawl up the tight mountain road, slowing almost to a standstill the higher it got. At the summit, the whole bus rocked like a see-saw: the front end went down, the back end rose and we began our descent to the north coast.

A wall of cloud hung like a floppy fringe over the fishing village of Garachico hundreds of feet below. I'd been to Garachico before, on one of our rare days out with Joy, David and Faith in the early days of the Smugglers. It had been our first taste of the real Tenerife and that day had stuck in my mind as an oasis of happiness in a desert of stress.

Garachico is famous for two things. It's home to the island's most popular, and often most wave-bashed, rock pools, a series of swimming holes that nature has carved out of the craggy seafront. It's also the only town on Tenerife that has been damaged by a volcanic eruption. So far.

Local legend has it that in 1706 a tyrannical Catholic priest who had become too big for his own cassock was cast out of the affluent town for abusing his position. Doing what, the history books don't say. He was a Catholic priest. I'll leave that to your imagination. Stomping away from the town, he stopped, turned and uttered the fateful words:

'*Garachico, pueblo rico,*
　　Gastadero de dinero,
　　Mal risco te caiga encima!'
　　(Garachico, rich town,
　　Waster of wealth,
　　Let an evil rock fall on you!)

Conveniently for the priest, but not so much for the towns-folk, evil rocks did fall a few days later. One of Mount Teide's volcanic offshoots had flared in anger, smothering the town and harbour in a river of molten lava. While the priest hid in a cave and gloated, much of Garachico was destroyed, and its trading prosperity abruptly came to an end.

As the bus neared the town of Icod de los Vinos, barren was replaced by bougainvillea, and the soft scents of lemon trees and lavender wafted through the open windows. Because it's a public service, TITSA's routes slice straight through the heart of towns such as this, giving passengers a view of the really 'real' Tenerife as locals buy meat from the tiny butchers', lay out brooms and bird cages in front of dark, dusty hardware shops, or just chat in the shade of expansive laurel trees and jab gnarled walking sticks at those they either don't recognise or don't care for.

As the bus stopped in traffic, the green wooden shutters of one roadside house flew open beside me. I glanced into the dark interior. I was close enough to make out faded figures in framed black and white photographs grouped on a dark wooden dining table, close enough to make out the intricate needlework on its lace tablecloth, and close enough to see the indignant expression of an aged lady staring back at me from a worn armchair. We held each other's gaze until the bus hissed and laboured forward.

Much like the house I was caught peering into, the town itself had done little to prettify itself. First impressions were unappealing, especially from inside the number 352, and yet every day the town sees hundreds of badly dressed tourists spilling from coaches and crowding into a particular leafy church plaza. The reason? To marvel at a thousand-year-old dragon tree that seeps blood.

Okay, maybe it's not actual blood, and nor is it associated with any fire-breathing beasts for that matter. But the tree is revered. Its bright red sap is still used to treat a host of medical unpleasantries in the Canaries, including stomach problems and skin infections.

As if bleeding dragon trees weren't enough, this 'unremarkable' town hides another remarkable secret – the Cueva del Viento. A labyrinth of volcanic tubes and caves snakes underground for over eleven miles, said to be the longest such complex in the world. Pretty big news if speleology rocks your world, and let's face it, whose world doesn't it rock, if we really dig deep?

In fact, for volcanologists, Tenerife is a veritable Disneyland. Mount Teide, which looms over Icod de los Vinos and is visible from many more distant parts of the island, kicks volcano ass in several ways. At over 12,000 feet above sea level, it's Spain's highest peak, but add to that the 13,000 feet of it underwater that you can't see and it becomes the third largest volcano on the planet (the largest two are both in Hawaii).

If you happen to be a subscriber to the International Association of Volcanology and Chemistry of the Earth's Interior's (IAVCEI) – a definite candidate for the planet's most unsexy moniker – you would know that since the 1990s Mount Teide has been included in a global list of sixteen 'decade volcanoes'. Not to provoke alarm where none is due (yet), but decade volcanoes are considered the most dangerous in the world. To be included in this roll of infamy, a volcano has to tick the following three boxes:

☐ Has exhibited a huge, hazardous and destructive eruption in the past

☐ Is in a populated area that could put tens of thousands of people at risk

☐ Has had lots of recent volcanic and seismic activity

Naturally, being on the A-list of celebrity volcanoes, Mount Teide is now monitored by some of the most sophisticated equipment available. However, big beasts are unpredictable. The only thing that *is* certain is that it's not a question of *if* Mount Teide will blow its top again, but *when*.

As I gazed through the window at the cone towering above Icod de los Vinos, a cloud formed above its peak. Or was it a cloud? I hoped it wouldn't spoil a nice bus ride.

An hour and a half after leaving Los Gigantes, the bus driver pulled into Puerto de la Cruz, a one-time fishing village that became Tenerife's old lady of tourism. This was the island's first resort area and is still favoured by holidaymakers looking for less busyness and more refinement than they would find in the racy south.

The metamorphosis began in the early nineteenth century, when British steamships offloaded the first wave of tourists keen to partake of the archipelago's healthy climate, as prescribed by stiff-collared doctors back home. Subsequent visitors to these northern shores included Agatha Christie and the Beatles.

Agatha Christie wasn't in the best of spirits when she came to Tenerife in 1927, aged thirty-six. Her mother had recently died and the marriage to her first husband had failed. The island must have proved a suitable tonic. While here she managed to finish two pieces of writing – *The Man from the Sea* and *The Mystery of the Blue Train.*

The Beatles came for ten days of downtime in May 1963. Well, three of them came – Paul, George and Ringo. John chose to holiday in Barcelona with band manager Brian Epstein. They offered to perform at the oceanfront San Telmo Lido nightclub, but its owner, wary of General Franco's disdain of all things liberal or cheery, declined. Instead, the trio went swimming...

and that was nearly the end of the Beatles as we know them. Paul got caught in the notoriously strong currents off Martiánez Beach and was swept out to sea. Thankfully, the ocean returned him and, after stern words with George and Ringo for having ignored his frantic waves, the Beatles' history continued.

Agatha Christie was also aware of the dangers of swimming off Martiánez Beach and wrote about it in her autobiography. She stated, rather dramatically, it must be said, 'Masses of people had been drowned there. It was impossible to get into the sea and swim; that could only be done by one or two of the very strongest swimmers, and even one of those had been drowned the year before.' Writers, eh? How they *do* exaggerate!

Anyways, back to my bus journey to Canarian integration... I was due to catch the half-hourly number 101 to Santa Cruz, nicknamed 'the stopping bus' for reasons that quickly became apparent. It set off with a full complement of passengers. And then stopped again almost before the doors had fully closed. It lurched forward a few hundred feet, then the doors hissed open again. And so it went on, this pattern continuing until we reached La Orotava, where the bus mysteriously emptied.

La Orotava is a city of two halves. The upper reaches comprise cobbled roads lined with ornate mansions parading white, yellow or burnt-amber facades. The lower half is given over to the more mundane – a profusion of shoe shops and insurance offices. If you ever stop in La Orotava, make sure you walk uphill – unless, of course, you're seeking shiny leather footwear or are looking to provide financial peace of mind to those you leave behind.

The stopping bus continued – or rather 'stopped' – all the way north to the capital, Santa Cruz, via La Laguna, Tenerife's second city and a moderately buzzy university town, part cobbled and historic but mostly jumbled and mercantile.

Santa Cruz terminus was exactly how bus stations should be – expansive, shiny and alive with frenzied to-ing and fro-ing – a warehouse of travel options. I had half an hour to kill before my next bus, the 264, which would take me to Almáciga, a remote village on the far side of the Anaga mountains at Tenerife's northern tip. If the genuine Canaries were to be found anywhere, it was probably in an isolated community unsoiled by the grubby hands of tourism.

But first it was time to eat. Bus-station fodder worldwide always has a distinctive flavour. Perhaps it's the subtle seasoning of diesel fumes, but my hot cheese and ham baguette didn't disappoint.

There's something else that's a standard feature of bus stations worldwide. They're frequented by curious characters not found in any other setting. And one of them was standing behind me in the queue as the 264 pulled in. I say 'behind', but the bearded vagrant stood that close that I felt I was wearing him. I could feel hot breath on the back of my neck, and as I shuffled a few inches further away, the breath followed.

I glanced left and right to see if anyone else was observing this strange behaviour, but other travellers milled around blissfully unbothered by this walking growth stuck to my back. I wanted to *feel* more Canarian, not have one attached to me.

Somewhat inevitably, my appendage followed me onto the

bus and sat next to me, from where he spent the entire fifty-minute ride beaming at me like he'd just found a new wife. I tried to ignore him, Canarian style, but realised I hadn't yet shaken the British in me and smiled back.

At San Andrés, a fishing village on the fringes of Santa Cruz, the bus turned into the hills, motoring higher and higher up a mountain road that scored the verdant slopes like a giant helter-skelter. At every death-defying curve (and there were plenty), our whistling driver hooted out a warning tune of symphonic grandeur to oncoming traffic, which was just as well, as this road too was hopelessly inadequate for two-directional encounters.

Then suddenly it went dark, and we emerged from a tunnel onto the north coastline. Near the frothing ocean below, clumps of white cottages lay like scattered sugar cubes on a green baize. The bus wound its way down to Almáciga, nothing more than a cluster of painted houses laced with narrow alleyways. The driver expertly reversed the big green bus into a wide footpath, turned off the engine, put his feet on the dashboard, and closed his eyes.

As my husband and I alighted, he lost interest in me and lolloped off inland, presumably to attach himself to some other lifeform. I walked down to the coastal road, where pavement blackboards offered fresh seafood and frosty refreshments at a trio of oceanfront cafes.

Armed with a plate of squid and boiled potatoes, some crusty bread and a local beer from the Restaurante Olga, I sat watching a couple of locals surf the waves that pounded the craggy coastline. I was at the furthest point possible from Playa de las Américas, Tenerife's epicentre of commercialism; sixty-two miles, to be exact. I was separated from civilisation by 3,000-foot-high mountains behind and a turbulent sea in front, and there was not a 'lucky-lucky man' selling fake watches and sunglasses to be seen. It was a perfect escape from the madding crowds and represented 'the other side' of Tenerife that the tourist board were now keen to promote.

I was so enamoured with Almáciga that I decided I would extend my stay. A handwritten note pinned behind the bar advertised rooms for rent. Fuelled by adventure adrenaline and three bottles of Dorada Especial, I waited for the bar person to return so I could make enquiries.

A couple walked in and announced, '*Buenas tardes*,' (Good afternoon) to no one in particular. From behind a newspaper in the corner, a voice called back, '*Buenas*.'

I liked this practice of strangers publicly greeting each other when they came into a bar or similar meeting place. It seemed friendly, retro and community-spirited. I'd noticed it in other local bars and restaurants and I decided that I would do the same from now on.

A leather-faced gentleman in a battered trilby sauntered in and slammed a coin on the bar. '*Hola*,' he muttered in a nicotine-gruff voice.

Nobody replied. It was my chance. '*Bolas*,' I shouted confidently into the silence. The silence became even quieter.

He looked at me, eyes narrowed. '*Qué?*'

In a rush of enthusiasm, I had combined the two customary responses – '*Buenas*' and '*Hola*' – into one word, unfortunately a word that meant 'balls' in Spanish. I just smiled, my cheeks a shade rosier.

The man muttered something and jabbed a finger into my chest. Thankfully, the bar lady returned and barked at the man before the situation escalated. My bubble popped, I decided that I was leaping the gun in my attempts at integration; instead of booking a room, I headed back to the bus stop. In the words of a previous – and exasperated – Spanish teacher, *poco a poco* assimilation was a more realistic approach than trying to do a full-throttle nosedive.

I boarded the 246 back to the bustle of Santa Cruz, changed onto the 110 express for the east-coast motorway run to Las Américas and re-entered the familiar world that I'd left eight hours before, a little deflated but not downhearted.

Back at the house, I regaled Joy with tales of my island adventure, enthusing about this 'other' side of Tenerife. She responded with adequate expressions, but I could tell she didn't share my excitement.

'You should write it down,' she said from behind a *Hello!* magazine. 'I bet other people would be interested.'

I noted the emphasis on 'other'.

CHAPTER TWELVE

The original inhabitants of Tenerife were called Guanches: cave dwellers who remained stuck in the Stone Age for perhaps longer than they should have. Their provenance is uncertain, but the most accepted theory suggests they arrived from North Africa in around 200 BC. Carbon dating of the sparse archaeological relics backs up this notion, as does the fact that there are similarities between the language and place names of the Canary Islands and those of the North African Berbers.

However, one rather large hole in this theory prevails – how did they get here? The Canary Islands were never connected to the African mainland, even though they're only sixty miles apart at the closest point (between the island of Fuerteventura and the most south-westerly tip of Morocco), and not a scrap of evidence has been found to suggest that the Guanches had any seafaring knowledge or indeed knew how to make boats.

Other anthropologists point to Mexico or Egypt as the root, based on similarities between the house-sized pyramids in Güímar, an otherwise unremarkable town (though with an excellent

museum) on Tenerife's dusty east coast, and the fact that the
Guanches also mummified their dead.

Those with vivid imaginations or a taste for mind-altering
chemicals have a more romantic theory about Tenerife's first
dwellers. They say that the Canary Islands are the highest peaks
of the fabled land of Atlantis and that the Guanches were the
only survivors when that continent inconveniently sank.

Either way, there aren't many true Guanches left on the island, despite claims to the contrary by stick-wielding shepherds
and others with similarly enduring careers. When the Spanish
conquered the islands in the fifteenth century, many islanders
were killed, or sold into slavery and shipped to Africa, Spain or
Italy. The genetic line of those that remained became diluted
through 'relationships' with their conquerors and other visiting
nationals. Nowadays, if you hear an islander proclaiming, '*Soy
Guanche*,' they're probably either drunk, misguided or referring
to a very tiny trace of the Guanche gene that's embedded deep
in their DNA.

Twenty-first-century Tenerife has a population of one million. Of that one million, roughly ten per cent are expats from
114 different countries. Contrary to popular belief, there are
actually more Italian expats on the island than anyone else. The
British make up only 18 per cent of the expat community, putting
them in third place, after the Germans.

According to figures from the Ministry of Employment and
Social Security, at the time of going to print there are also 678
Irish living here, 169 Americans, sixteen Canadians and twelve
Australians. There's also one person from Azerbaijan. I hope for

his or her sake that they speak Spanish, or they may be in for a lonely time.

Add to that the five million visiting holidaymakers each year, two million of them British, and it's hardly surprising that Tenerife is a cosmopolitan cauldron of different cultures. Like ourselves when we arrived, pale-faced and wide-eyed, in 1991, many of these visitors fall into the bracket of 'baffled and bemused'; fish out of water in a strange land they know nothing about and surrounded by strange people of whom they have no understanding. Particularly if they're from Azerbaijan.

It was these baffled and bemused of Tenerife – expats and visitors alike – that interested me most. I became fascinated with the mismatching of cultures on our island and I began to jot down my observations. Incomers from northern Europe often had a particularly confusing time of it: being used to efficiency, over-politeness and logical reasoning, they were completely flummoxed when faced with the laissez-faire, often abrupt and always *mañana* attitude of Tenerifians.

As my interest grew, these notes about life in Tenerife became more detailed, and dare I say it, more organised. I even bought a Moleskine notebook, which made me feel very writerly. Joy and a few others read the notes and commented that I should try and get them published. This is the literary equivalent of your mum filling in the forms for *X Factor* after hearing you sing in the shower. However, with more than a little trepidation, I decided to dip a toe into the world of published writing and sent off a couple of 700-word expat observations to *Island Connections*, the main local English-language newspaper in Tenerife, which came out once a fortnight.

I received a polite email back thanking me for my contributions and informing me that they would appear in consecutive editions the following month. Hell, I was going to be published! A real newspaper had deemed my words worthy of their twenty thousand readers!

Little did I realise that the editors of pretty much all the local rags were desperate for words to fill the gaps between advertisements and advertorials. Any string of ink in a reasonable state of cohesion would have been accepted. But I wasn't to know that and duly celebrated my literary breakthrough as if I'd won the Booker Prize.

As if that wasn't victory enough, the initial email was followed up with further correspondence asking if I'd like to become a columnist, providing 'witty' observations for every fortnightly edition. I felt my career was racing: from random note-scribbler to columnist in the space of a few weeks! Naturally for a local paper, the rewards weren't overly generous. In fact, there weren't any. Not in spendables anyway. I *was* allowed to place a free advert in the classifieds, if I could think of anything to advertise. The ad value was worth the equivalent of around £7 at the time, which priced my work at a penny a word.

I had no reason to question this rate. Mainly because I had nothing to compare it with. Within twelve months, however, this would become £1 a word. And I still find it hard to believe how fortune enabled such a rapid rise.

Several weeks later, I was invited to visit the basement office of said newspaper in Los Cristianos. Kandy, the editor, asked if I'd be interested in a part-time job, working in the features department. I looked around the office to try and identify the journalistic colleagues I'd be working alongside.

'Who's in that department?' I asked.

'Julie does the features at the moment.' Kandy nodded towards a short, rotund figure at the far side of the office.

Julie was mechanically shoving Rich Tea biscuits in her mouth at an impressive rate.

'But she's on maternity leave soon. Besides which, she's crap.' Kandy waved and smiled; 'Aren't you, Julie?'

Julie waved back cheerily.

Life at the paper, albeit only part-time, was fun and varied. Kandy had handed the editorial reins to Bridget, a fiercely patriotic Irish girl with actual experience in reporting. She had worked for RTE radio and studied journalism at university. Happily, she had a similar sense of humour and was happy for me to continue producing my columns on life in Tenerife, in between doing bits of more serious newsgathering.

Newsgathering at *Island Connections* did not involve pounding the streets with notepad stuffed in deep pockets; rather, it entailed nothing more adventurous than scanning the daily Spanish papers and translating items that were either of interest to Tenerife readers or, more importantly as far as Bridget was concerned, contained some reference to Ireland. Daniel O'Donnell, Roy Keane and *Lord of the Dance* were given many more column inches than they deserved. Those inches may not have been entirely accurate either. My Spanish was still about the level of a five-year-old's and despite me spelling this out to

Bridget, I was handed all the translation work. The bits I didn't get, which was most of them, I guessed or made up. But at least it helped to fill the paper, which was the overriding objective.

As Bridget's confidence in me grew, I was landed with more lofty commissions, such as writing the horoscopes. I know some people take these predictions very seriously, but for me, assigning fate was a random affair. One edition, Pisces would be urged to 'think about your next move to take that extra step towards self-fulfilment', while Leos would be advised 'not to make any hasty decisions as that may lead to stress'. Six weeks later, destinies would be reversed: Pisces would be advised to 'think long and carefully about an impending decision that could lead to upset', while it would be Leos' turn to 'start pondering what to do next to achieve personal ambitions'. I doubt anyone noticed, nor cared for that matter. Horoscopes are designed to be ambiguous enough so that any situation can be shoe-horned in to fit the forecast.

Occasionally real news would have to be investigated: murders that couldn't be ignored, local political scandals that needed exposing, visits by fading celebrities who had to be interviewed. Back then, in 2001, Tenerife was not exactly awash with paparazzi desperate to catch the ugly side of stardom. We had plenty of ugly, just not many visiting celebs. Michael Jackson had performed in Santa Cruz in 1993, and a handful of other stars have graced our volcanic shores since, but the island certainly wasn't, and still isn't a key player in the world pop-music scene.

Icon-hungry islanders were fed only small crumbs of pop stardom, acts from the eighties trying to squeeze the last drops of adulation from long-gone recording careers, like Kajagoogoo or Shakin' Stevens. On very rare occasions, the dying embers of their careers would suddenly spark briefly into life again, such as with Spandau Ballet.

Tony Hadley had been booked to perform to backing tracks at a monthly eighties disco and I was dispatched to interview him. It was at the time when he had very publicly fallen out with the rest of the band and I was waved out of the office by Bridget early one afternoon with the words 'See what you can get out of him' ringing in my ears. Tony, as I like to call him, was notoriously candid, and I knew that I was in for some juicy backbiting and scandalous name-calling. Unfortunately, it would never make it to print.

The interview had been arranged for 3pm on the terrace of Brinsley Forde's bar. Brinsley was the former singer of reggae success Aswad. With his immense musical talent, Rasta philosophy and pop-world connections, he had decided a small cocktail bar in the middle of Playa de las Américas was the next logical step in his musical ascendancy. He did make a mean Sex on the Beach cocktail though, so I guess all was not lost.

The first thing that I noticed about Tony Hadley was his presence. Some people effortlessly ooze star status. Dressed in black shirt, jeans and cowboy boots and standing over six feet tall, Tony was one of them. I was feeling more than a little awestruck, stuttering out my questions, so the arrival of a tropical, fruit-laden loosener was a welcome interruption. As soon as the glasses were empty, two more magically appeared.

Thanks to the alcohol, relaxation kicked in, quickly followed

by complete and utter inebriation. Before long we were calling
each other 'mate'. On my side, this was because it seemed pretty
cool to be on 'mate' terms with a (once) legendary pop star. With
Tony, I'm pretty sure that he'd just plain forgotten my name half
an hour into the interview.

Afternoon became early evening, the sun casting a golden
glow across the ocean behind us. By now I had all but aban-
doned lengthy note-taking, making the journalistic decision to
just let the friendly conversation flow and see where it took
us. I nonchalantly scribbled down the odd word while noisily
hoovering the last remnants of rum through a straw, but I knew
that I needed nothing more than the barest reminders to be able
to produce scintillating copy in the morning. As the interview
came to an end with an exchange of manly backslapping, some
four hours and half a dozen cocktails after it had begun, I realised
that walking required a great deal more attention than I usually
afforded it.

I sat forlornly at my desk the following morning, nursing a
rusty head and staring at a notepad that alarmingly contained
nothing but abstract words: 'deal', 'his wife', 'Norwich', 'last
year' and something that looked like it might have said 'custard'.
None of it made the slightest bit of sense. Not one word triggered
any memory of even part of the conversation.

There was only one thing to do. I searched the internet for
every recent interview Tony had given and cobbled together a
thousand words from those reports. It wasn't my finest hour,
but, still, I had a nice photo of him and me together, and it was
with a modicum of satisfaction that I heard he'd looked just as

much the worse for wear as I had that morning.

Being arrested in the name of journalistic endeavours was also not one of my finest moments and could easily have been avoided had I been blessed with even a smattering of media knowledge.

There was a local news story gaining pace about the national police in Playa de las Américas and I was duly commanded to get a picture of a police station to accompany our report. What Bridget failed to advise was discretion. So, when the camera was snatched out of my hand and both arms twisted up my back in a manner I neither appreciated nor was accustomed to, I was a little taken aback.

I had been standing in the middle of a roundabout in front of the police station trying to decide whether a portrait or landscape image would work best when I noticed movement out of the corner of my eye. Just as I turned to investigate, I was grabbed by both arms, frogmarched in front of a queue of halted traffic, bundled through a metal side door and pushed into a plastic chair in an interview room.

The ETA terrorist group, intent on forcing an independent Basque state, had recently been on a bombing spree on the mainland, which understandably had put all Spanish police stations on full alert, even those in the remotest territories. Taking photos of police stations at such a time was liable to cause a little concern amongst those in uniform and it was three such individuals who were forcefully enquiring why I'd been doing it.

'Name,' barked the most senior. He stood up, rolled up his

sleeves and leant over the desk.

I bleated my name.

'Who are you working for?' Thankfully, his English was impeccable.

'*Island Connections.*'

Boss policeman's eyes opened wider. I felt the two lackeys who had strong-armed me move closer. 'Which island connections? Give me names.'

'Err, Bridget, Kandy...'

'Write this down,' instructed the boss to one of his lackeys. 'So, these connections on the island, what do they do?'

This was not going in the direction I had anticipated. I needed to backtrack fast, but before I could, the policeman changed tack. He clicked through the digital images on my camera.

'Why are you taking photos of this police station and my officers?' He leant in. I could smell garlic, stale tobacco and a faint whiff of whisky.

'My boss asked me to shoot them.' I knew at the very moment the word 'shoot' fell from my trembling lips that a hole the size of Calcutta had just opened beneath me.

The chief looked at his two sidekicks, said something in Spanish and dispatched one of them through the door behind me. I smiled weakly at the chief, who glared through narrow eyes as he sparked a shiny silver Zippo lighter, took a slow intake of nicotine and let the smoke drift out from his nose and mouth. The lighter was similar to one I'd given my brother on his last birthday, but I decided not to share that observation just then.

The door opened and a new interviewer came in. He wore dark blue trousers that concertinaed above scuffed black shoes. His matching jacket strained at the shoulders and waist as he bent forward. His neck spilled in pink folds over a dandruff-speckled collar. He turned to eye me as the chief filled him in.

Fortunately, he was a little more astute at identifying international terrorists than his colleagues. He must have been a lot busier too and thus was less inclined to try and find a career-boosting headline crime where there was none. Ignoring the revelations of the chief, he sighed, picked up the camera and deleted all the shots of the police station.

'Take any more photos like that and you'll find yourself in a cell. Understand?' He thrust the camera into my chest, ordered the chief to let me go and hurried out of the office.

CHAPTER THIRTEEN

I pondered my run-in with the authorities as I drove home later that day. It was a reminder that having no journalistic background meant I was always going to be vulnerable to falling foul of the law. It also served to highlight the fact that I loved writing, but only when left alone to do it my way.

I unlocked the front door as quietly as I could and pushed it open just enough to poke my head in. Fugly, although still only the size of a large rat, had taken to ambushing whoever walked through the door, with Joy the exception. This self-appointed role of protector wasn't such an issue if the victim was wearing long trousers, but today was hot, and I wasn't.

However, we had discovered that Fugly was slightly deaf. If you entered with stealth and guile, lacerations of the shins and calves could be avoided, or at least minimised. I looked left through the kitchen doorway, then right, to scan the living room. Through the open patio doors I could see Joy taking in the evening sun on the raised concrete plinth above the garden. Her feet were perched on a white plastic chair and she was reading a magazine, possibly *Hello!*, possibly *Bella*. It was hard to tell. Just as it was hard to tell whether the white fluffy object under her chair was Fugly or a discarded head towel. I decided it was Fugly and strode through the living room and onto the patio.

Joy turned round and beamed. 'Good day?' she enquired.

'Well... different,' I said. 'Beer?' I bent down to give Fugly a stroke under the chair. A bold move, particularly when I realised it was a towel after all. I took a sharp intake of breath. Out of the corner of my eye I caught a flash of white. Twisting my head, I just had time to see our psychotic cat charging at me on two feet, front paws boxing the air like a miniature bare-knuckle fighter.

The time it took to stand up was exactly the time it took for Fugly to lunge and scrape three lines of blood from my right calf.

'Get the... off, you sodding psycho,' I said, shaking my leg as I tried to avoid a repeat assault from the hissing banshee. 'Joy, tell her.'

Joy draped a hand over the chair. 'Fuglyyyyy, sch-sch-sch,' she said, as though cooing at a baby. Fugly ceased immediately and started to rub against Joy's fingers.

'That cat is seriously deranged,' I said.

'It's just her way of saying welcome home, Daddy.' Joy laughed and rose from the chair. 'I'll get the cream, you make friends.'

I flopped into Joy's chair, keeping one eye on Fugly, who was licking her paws, savouring the taste of blood and victory. The magazine Joy had been reading was open at an interview with Bill Bryson, a travel writer whose very book I was enjoying at the time. Although he was born and raised in America, the author's dry, self-deprecating humour was more akin to the British way of looking at the world. His was one of the few books I'd read that made me chuckle out loud.

In the interview, Bill mentioned that he had become a patron of the children's charity Barnardo's and that he would be accompanying hikers on a sponsored trek in Peru, a country that had always fascinated me. There were thirty-two places available on the sponsored challenge – perhaps Joy and I could take two of them...? After my brush with the law and subsequent mauling by Fugly, strolling with my favourite author in a far-off land suddenly seemed to be just what was needed.

I showed Joy the article as she handed me a beer and the antiseptic cream.

'I know, I've read it. I left it open to show you. That's who you're reading at the moment, isn't it?'

I jumped straight in. 'Do you fancy going?'

'To Peru? Me? Trudging up mountains? Camping in a tent? Err, let me think about it. No.'

'I've always wanted to go to Peru,' I said. I gazed longingly at the full-page image of Machu Picchu, the lost city in the Amazon jungle.

'Go then.'

'Seriously?'

'Seriously. Why not?' We've got the money. Trekking with your favourite writer, an adventure in a country you've always said you wanted to visit. All for a good cause. Go!'

It had been comfortably appealing when it was just a yearning. Now that it was a genuine possibility, the thought scared me. My mind went into overdrive. Was this just a ploy for Joy to get rid of me for three weeks? Was she in touch with Steve again, my ex-best friend with whom she'd had an affair during the darkest of our bar days? Was this the perfect opportunity for a repeat of her own sordid adventures?

I shook my head. These doubts still surfaced occasionally, a reminder that the circle of trust still hadn't completely healed. Perhaps it never would. Many nights I'd pondered the issue. To assume that you could always trust your partner completely, no matter the circumstances, was presumptuous and naive. It meant that you didn't have to try as hard at the relationship. It was lazy and I couldn't afford to risk that again.

I'd vowed to banish the flashbacks and suspiciousness from my mind. Though I wasn't so foolish as to wallow in the misguided luxury of thinking it could never happen again, it was also difficult to fully forget. Three and a half years had passed since I'd found Joy and Steve wrapped around each other in the Smugglers kitchen, but when the memories ambushed me, they were as clear as if it had been yesterday. I pushed the thoughts aside. It was the only way to fully repair our relationship. We had to put things behind us and focus on the future. But sometimes that was easier said than done.

'I'm afraid all of the places are taken now,' said the lady at the end of the phone.

'Oh,' I said forlornly. 'Okay.' The disappointment of not being able to trek the highlands of Peru with my hero-in-print was lightened by knowing that I wouldn't have to leave my cosy nest.

'I can put your name on the waiting list if you like?' continued the voice. 'If somebody drops out, you'd be fourth in line.'

I agreed but knew in my heart that the chance of not one but four people having second thoughts or becoming ill or injured was slim to say the least.

Which is why it came as something of a surprise when I received a phone call two months later to say there was now a space free and would I like to take it.

Would I like to take it? The lady was asking if I'd like to trek through the jungle to one of the world's greatest discoveries side-by-side with my literary hero, Bill Bryson. Was she mad? Did she really need to ask?

My late enrolment meant I had only three months until departure. On May 19th I was to meet up with thirty-one similarly well-intentioned individuals. We would fly together from Madrid to Lima, then travel on to Cuzco for a four-day high-altitude trek to Machu Picchu, the ancient Inca ruins perched high in the Peruvian Andes. Before then, I had to raise the minimum sponsorship money that would allow me to take part. And I had to get fit, as the full-day treks would take us up steep ascents to mountain peaks of over 13,000 feet above sea level. Along the way we would encounter hazards more normally associated with *Indiana Jones* films, such as altitude sickness, malaria-carrying mosquitoes, insta-death snakes and many, many other delights.

All of this had seemed very exciting and adventurous on the

pages of Joy's magazine, but now, as reality loomed, I had to admit to a certain trepidation. Panic buttons had been pushed on three fronts – sponsorship, training and remaining alive.

As far as sponsorship went, I had to raise a minimum of £2,500, and in true Tenerifian spirit, everything was now needed at the last moment. A clutch of local businesses had generously pledged support, but I was in urgent need of further backing. We had plenty of money in the bank, so if push came to shove, I could quite easily have covered the sponsorship amount myself, but from Barnardo's point of view, it wasn't just about the funding, it was about raising awareness of their charity and sparking long-term interest in their cause. I'd decided that I would 'sponsor' myself to the tune of £500, and I'd obviously cover all clothes, equipment and the extra expenses of getting myself to the departure point from Tenerife, but I still needed to badger almost £2,000 out of friends, family and colleagues at *Island Connections*. I concluded that now was not the time to resign from my job.

However, the initial reaction to my endeavours to collect money for my trip typically went something like this:

'Would you like to sponsor me on behalf of Barnardo's?'

'Sponsor you for what exactly?'

'Well, I need to raise £2,500 to go on a trek to Peru.'

Momentary pause and a narrowing of eyes.

'You mean you want me to pay towards your holiday?'

Here would begin a long explanation of how they would not be paying for my holiday but instead contributing money that the charity would not otherwise get.

'Well why don't I give the money straight to charity then?' they'd persist.

The truth was, this was new income for the charities. As the special events manager for Barnardo's told me in a subsequent phone call when I raised the issue, 'The adventure brings the money and the supporter. This is new money and new support for Barnardo's and we wouldn't be able to raise this money without the pull of the adventure.'

After paying for administration, flights, accommodation, meals, English-speaking guides, local ground-handlers, a doctor, back-up support, mechanics, vehicles, and event organisation, the charity receive around 52 to 53 per cent of the minimum sponsorship target and 100 per cent of any further amount raised.

I was informed that over the past few years Barnardo's had benefited to the tune of £1.3 million from such challenges, a substantial proportion of the events department's income. The challenges also attracted new supporters to the charity, as the special events manager explained: 'Most people who trek with us are new to Barnardo's and go on to support the charity in many ways after their trip. Also, every person who treks then tells friends, family and colleagues as well as local press, so the awareness of what Barnardo's is and what we do is increased significantly every time we recruit a new trekker.'

It made sense to me and I renewed my efforts to cajole cash from those around me with all the zeal of an African missionary. However, although I was convinced of the moral argument, others were not. It was only the generosity of my mum and stepfather Jack that salvaged my campaign. They offered two weeks' use of their apartment on El Beril as a prize in a raffle I had devised. *Island Connections* graciously allowed me to advertise the contest in consecutive editions of the paper, which boosted the coffers to a level acceptably close to my minimum.

On the training front, the four-day Machu Picchu trail was graded moderate-to-hard and the organisers had advised us that unless we were in seriously good shape, we would struggle. We would be walking at heights of over 10,000 feet, and there would be a certain amount of jungle-wading. At the least, trekking at that altitude would cause breathlessness and dizzy spells; if we were physically unprepared, such symptoms could develop into something a little more serious – death, for instance.

CHAPTER FOURTEEN

'Trek training' began in earnest a week after I received my join-up call – and ended the following day.

A certain amount of surprise accompanied Joy's decision to be my hiking buddy in Teide National Park. Joy is the kind of person who believes that if God had intended us to walk, he wouldn't have created air-conditioning for cars. But she was adamant that I needed to be able to keep up with Bill Bryson if I was to make the most of the experience.

Our first walk was going to be a gentle breaking in, so we chose the route around Los Roques, a protrusion of volcanic rocks extending from the desiccated plains of Tenerife's central Las Cañadas crater next to Mount Teide volcano. It was also close to the visitors centre bar, the idea being that the promise of a celebratory Martini and Sprite would act as the proverbial carrot while we trudged through dust and cacti.

Armed with a day-pack stuffed full of the usual necessities – water, camera, jumper, snacks and map – plus a few last-minute essentials added by Joy – mobile phone, wet wipes and lipstick

– we strode purposefully past a coach-load of Italian tourists. They'd just arrived and had immediately set about enlivening the mountain quiet with their raucous babble. They began to arrange themselves into a photo scrum. '*Ahh, bella, bellissima...*' they continually exclaimed about the desert scenery, kissing each other and any woolly-hatted trekker that happened to venture too close.

The Los Roques route is a circular walk around a clutch of monoliths in the huge red and ochre Las Cañadas caldera, the kind of landscape you'd more associate with the Lone Ranger than a holiday resort. It was graded 'easy' by the map we were using and was supposed to take about two and a half hours.

After just twenty minutes of kicking up clouds of orange-red dust under the shadow of solitary fingers of rock, we had eaten 75 per cent of our snacks and finished off 50 per cent of our water. 'These columns are volcanic plugs,' I explained to Joy, reading from the guidebook. 'They're formed after an eruption leaves a hardened head of rock over the vent, a bit like a scab that forms over a squeezed spot.'

Joy looked at me, her face lacking any discernible emotion. 'I think I'll ring my mum,' she said.

I marched on as she burst into animated conversation on speakerphone, discussing who had said what to who, giving suggestions on how to alleviate cousin Benjamin's niggling bowel problems, and comparing what the two of them had eaten for the last three decades. Million-year-old rock formations passed by, plants that had struggled for centuries to eke out an existence continued to eke without a hint of sympathy or appreciation, and views unmatched anywhere on the planet were ignored. But at least Joy was happy and was there with me – in body at least.

An hour later, above the scrunch of volcanic gravel, I heard the obligatory two or three false endings that women exchange to soften the blow of a conversation coming to a stop:

'Okay, got to go now, bye.'

'Okay, bye. Oh, just a quick one... remember Sue?'

'Sue?'

'You know Sue! Sue! Sue from up the road. Sue... married to Sydney. Blind. Always wore black. Sue.'

'Oh, black and blind Sue! What about her?'

'She died.'

'Oh!'

'Anyway, just wanted to tell you. Bye, love. Love you.'

'Bye, Mum. Love you.'

'Oh, before you go... what was the name of that programme where they all live on an estate?'

'*Brookside?*'

'Yes, that's the one.'

Pause.

'Why?'

'Nothing. Couldn't remember it. Okay... Take care... Bye.'

'Okay, better go, Joe's eyebrows are going into orbit. Bye, Mum.'

'Bye, love.'

'Bye.'

'Bye.'

'Yep... bye.'

'Bye.'

'Any news?' I said.

'Not really. She sends her love.'

For the remainder of the walk, we did share some monumental views of Mount Teide and its conjoined twin, Las Narices (The Nostrils), dominating the landscape against the cloudless blue sky. By the time we completed our circuit, despite a less than easy uphill finale, Joy's attitude had risen from a base of grumbling regret to a plateau of indifference. It was more than I had hoped for.

I'd anticipated that I'd need a few jabs for Peru, but the list, presented with more than a little glee by south Tenerife's only English GP, Dr Johnson, did nothing to reduce my anxiety levels. Malaria, Hepatitis A, Typhoid, Yellow Fever, Rabies, Dysentery, Dyslexia, Discomfort, Distress and a whole host of other disorders and disturbances were cheerily rhymed off.

Some of the vaccinations he could administer himself, but for the rest I was sent up to the Department of Tropical Diseases in Santa Cruz, where I also had to register the fact that I was travelling to a land of alien microbes.

I'm not sure why, but I expected the department to be like a military hospital, accessed via a fern-filled glass conservatory, creaking with exotic plants and patrolled by scientists in white coats silently marking observations on clipboards hidden from prying eyes.

I thought I might be settled in a cracked leather armchair in a dark study festooned with glass tanks and jars containing specimens of wildlife yet to be identified. The perils of journeying through deepest, darkest Peru would be spelled out in fatherly tones by an ambassadorial figure. He would sit calmly, pressing fingertips together as he regaled me with his own close encounters with flesh-eating diseases and flora that could swallow a man whole.

We would drink tea as he offered advice, guidance and an emergency phone number should I need more of his wisdom when being seasoned by cannibals, cornered by rabid tigers or caught in a jungle typhoon with nothing more than a box of matches, a Swiss Army knife and a clean pair of underpants.

It was nothing like that. The only air of mystery was provided by the young female receptionist whose midnight moustache and painfully thinning hair set my imagination into overdrive. Had she fallen foul of a potent virus that was, even now, advancing room by room through this cold, heartless building, turning women into men, boys into girls? She had my sympathy until she tried to fob me off in that peculiarly Canarian manner.

'Hello, can you tell me where I can find Dr Ramirez?'

From behind the high wooden reception counter she greeted me with a look that suggested I was trespassing. 'You can't see the doctor without an appointment. Good day.'

She turned and took a step back as she replaced a box folder on the row of shelves behind her. The virus had clearly got a firm hold of her. Her plain white blouse displayed the slim yet curvaceous upper body of a model, but her black and white checked trousers contained hips that were as wide as an Edwardian sideboard. It was obvious that two separate people had been joined at the waist.

I pulled the relevant card from a plastic folder I was holding. 'I have an appointment. Three o'clock, see?'

She stooped and peered at the card from a distance, then flicked her head in resignation. 'Third door on the left, second floor.'

For a second I thought my appointment might actually come close to the one I'd imagined. Dr Ramirez's room was small and dark. Its shelves were indeed lined with jars, but they contained inanimate objects like cotton pads, bandages and vacuum-wrapped needles, not oversized insects or pointy-toothed reptiles. The doc was wearing a white coat, though I suspected it was someone else's, someone with a much bigger frame than that of the short and wiry Dr Ramirez.

Alas, the conversation went no further than a perfunctory Q & A on where I was going and for how long, and what medication I was currently on. He offered no opinions on, insights into or even interest in my forthcoming travels, and after receiving jabs in various fleshy parts of my anatomy, I was dismissed without ceremony.

CHAPTER FIFTEEN

The time had come. I would be meeting my author hero. It was a dead heat between the excitement of foreign travel and making friends with unarguably the best author on the planet.

On the appointed day, I met the other like-minded experience-seekers in Madrid airport and after brief introductions to thirty-one strangers and two guides, I looked around for Bill Bryson. I'd already decided that the best policy would be to forego star-struck shyness and instead stride in with a purposeful introduction. Except I couldn't see him. Maybe he was joining us later. Maybe he was being pampered in the VIP lounge away from the riff-raff.

'Where's Bill Bryson?' I asked one of our guides eventually.

'Oh, he had to pull out at the last minute. Business in America. Sends his apologies and wishes you all well.'

Whaaaat? My heart sank. No Bill? I was devastated. All the build-up, all the thoughts of pal-ing up with a legend, sharing the journey, getting insights into his life and writerly secrets, gone in three short sentences.

I ambled aboard the twelve-hour flight to Lima with head and heart both heavy. My mood darkened to the point where only negativity remained. Fears of deep-vein thrombosis flashed through my mind as I remained folded into my personal two square feet of airspace for what seemed like a decade and a half. It was a decade and a half long enough to pull myself out of the disappointment and regain enthusiasm for what was going to be the trip of a lifetime. 'No more sulking, Mr Cawley,' I admonished myself.

Lima was not a very glamorous opener. There were bars across every window of our hotel, the toilets had locks that could have countered a prison break, and we were warned not to leave our accommodation unescorted, not to eat seafood or salad, and to avoid ice in our drinks. We were, of course, then served a welcome aperitif called Pisco Sour crammed with crushed ice, followed by a forbidden prawn cocktail with illegal salad garnish.

Cusco, the Inca capital and the starting point of the trek, would also take some getting used to. At 11,000 feet above sea level, it had character in abundance but was noticeably lacking in oxygen. So much so that something as exertive as scratching your head could cause a fit of breathlessness. We would spend two days in the city acclimatising to the thin air, and to Peruvian culture and customs.

Our stay in the city began with a memorable welcome. As the coach pulled up to drop us at our hotel, two identical women waved at us from a derelict plot facing our accommodation. Their ages were impossible to guess under the masses of red cloth and wrinkles. They bustled along the edge of the road, their voluminous claret skirts stirring dusty vapour trails behind. The waving continued, accompanied by toothless smiles, as they both crouched to watch us disembark from the coach. Peruvians, I decided, were nothing if not friendly. As slow streams of liquid trickled from beneath the folds of their frocks, I realised the real reason they were crouching. On the coach, hands that were waving, quickly dropped.

After dumping our luggage, we decided to explore the main Avenida del Sol thoroughfare, where crinkle-faced men waved bundles of notes at us, eager to exchange Peruvian soles for US dollars. Taxi drivers blared horns to attract our attention, pulling over to see if we wanted their services, and the rest of the traffic blared horns just because everyone else was. In the middle of every crossroads, white-helmeted policemen valiantly tried to impose some kind of order on the chaos, whistling and pointing indiscriminately as cars missed them by inches and shrouded them in swirls of blue and grey smoke.

Within hours, we met the infamous street kids of Cusco. At the Plaza de Armas, the historical centre of the city, a small boy approached, clutching a wad of postcards that bore faded, near-identical images of the square in which we stood.

'Meester, you buy?'

A threadbare poncho covered an even more threadbare shirt that had probably once been white. From beneath a fringe of ruffled black hair, tired eyes looked up, pleading with me to look.

'Five for one sol. Please, meester. Look, all different.'

There was absolutely no way I could refuse. I decided I would fire the cards off to Nan, who I knew would play them to her advantage in further games of Pensioner Top Trumps. I picked five and gave the boy a one-sol coin (worth about twenty pence at the time).

'*Gracias*,' he said, expressionless, before moving on to Ian, a computer worker from Scotland.

Within seconds, two more boys and a girl approached. They had the same pleading eyes, upturned palms and insistent whines. 'Pleeeaaaase!' they chorused in singsong tones. 'Why you not give me money? Why? Why?'

We gave them a coin each, but, like expert Tenerife timeshare salesmen, they moved in for the upsell. 'One more sol, meester. Please, meester. One more for me.'

We were beginning to get the picture now as we could see the next batch of six- and seven-year-olds lining up for the attack.

Back at the hotel, I braced myself for a traditional feast of guinea pig. I'd vowed to try it and thanked the waiter as he placed the scrawny leg on my plate. Earlier that day we'd seen fifteen of the critters in a pen at a village we were taken to – alive and relatively cute. This one was neither. The little claw gripped onto a potato in a last desperate attempt not to be eaten. What little meat I managed to scrape from its puny limb was a bit like rabbit with attitude. I flashed polite smiles of appreciation at our host, but I couldn't say it was a meal I'd want to repeat.

Finally, it was time for the trek itself: forty-five kilometres over four days, supported by fourteen local porters (*chasqui*), who would carry the tents, cooking utensils, camp essentials and our overnight bags. Many of our porters worked the fields and this income was an essential supplement during the visitor season. Nonetheless, we all felt a little awkward, seeing them hunched and shivering inside identical red- and yellow-embroidered ponchos as they waited for us at the 'Kilometre 82' start point, the sun yet to throw its warmth from beyond the distant snow-capped peaks. There was no way we could have done the trek without them: the terrain was challenging to say the least, and the altitude made everything that much harder.

We set off slowly, climbing and descending and climbing again, following the white rush of mountain rivers, creaking across rope bridges, slogging up unfeasibly muddy inclines, dodging low-hanging vines and tramping through dense jungle tangles. Small rabbit-like rodents (*viscachas*) played amongst the rocks, and hummingbirds hovered just long enough for lens caps to be removed.

On the lower slopes we came across occasional tiny settlements of three or four ramshackle wood and mud huts. We stopped at one. Smoke swirled from the doorway and, inside, the amber glow from a dying fire illuminated the face of a young boy sitting cross-legged and making the most of the heat. We stared at each other for a moment, both curious.

A larger hut served as a corner shop. The principal stock was alcohol, supplied in the form of beer bottles and cartons of Black Cat red wine. Alongside these were clear plastic bags of leaves, individual sheets of tin foil and a large stack of microwave stews. A blanket of dust covered the latter and would surely remain there unless future plans for the village included a supply of electricity.

The clear plastic bags were more in demand. They contained

cocaine. Well, not strictly cocaine, but the raw leaves from which cocaine is extracted. Unlike in Tenerife, where most drug deals are done with an element of discretion, in Cusco we had all been openly encouraged to buy a popcorn-bag of loose cocoa leaves from street vendors for about sixty pence and, for a further twenty pence, a pebble of lime ash. This combination would help counter the effects of high altitude.

Two of our group declined to buy or use the raw drugs, and unfortunately both would suffer as a consequence. Sue, a born-again Christian, refused the cocoa leaves on religious grounds, and she was the first to fall victim to altitude sickness. A sudden urgent shout of 'Doctor!' passed along our line of walkers a few hours into day one, and we pressed our backs to the bushes to allow him to pass. He and our guide sat her up and managed to revive her with water.

Steve, a marathon runner and undoubtedly the fittest amongst us, was the other trekker who didn't want to use the cocoa leaves, being a clean-health obsessive. To the surprise and alarm of all of us, he too fell prey to altitude sickness. As we approached the 13,780-foot summit of the uninvitingly named Woman's Pass on day two, Steve collapsed unconscious. A radio call was put out to the porters, who had already moved on to the next stop to prepare lunch. Within the hour, three *chasquis* had run back along the trail to take it in turns carrying Steve over their shoulders down to a lower altitude.

The rest of us continued, unable to cover more than a hundred paces at a time before light-headedness and the need to take in more oxygen forced us to rest. It seemed that my 'altitude training' with Joy in Tenerife had been no use at all.

The higher we climbed, the bleaker the scenery became. Instead of the chirrup of insects and the rustle of leaves, laboured footsteps on gravel and rock, gasps for breath and the pounding of my own heartbeat provided the soundtrack.

I was quite happy to turn to whatever substance was available whenever I felt the excruciating headaches taking hold. I'd duly dip into a pocket and wrap four or five leaves around a tiny scraping of lime ash to make a small parcel. This was then lodged between cheek and gums to allow the lime ash to react with one of the fourteen elements in the cocoa leaf, producing a chemical buzz and a numbing of the mouth. It tasted of very strong tea and was definitely effective in alleviating headaches or nausea. After half an hour or so, the leaves would break up, leaving speckles of green between your teeth. This became part of the 'trek look', along with a two- or three-day stubble, baggy eyes, and hair styled by Mother Nature.

Despite our battles with the altitude and the challenges that came with trekking and camping, there were many moments of perfection, particularly at night-time when dozens of tiny candle flames would dance throughout our field of tents. Lying head to head with a group who only days before had been complete strangers, we would share beer and rum and watch shooting stars in the diamond-encrusted charcoal sky, then fall asleep listening to the musical clicking of crickets, the howling of distant wolves and the gentle flow of nearby mountain streams.

Within a day's hike of Machu Picchu itself, we entered the Amazon rainforest proper. Sunshine sparkled on a cluster of small lakes extending like stepping stones to the vivid green canopy beyond. The trail grew narrower and more tangled, the green more intense. We wove through hand-cut stone corridors and tunnels of vines. In the distance, a rumbling announced the imminent arrival of a tropical storm. Within minutes it came roaring down. The trail became a treacherous, muddy slide. The hammering rain was funnelled directly onto us as we passed under patches of leafy spread. I cursed myself for having invested only £2.50 in a flimsy raincoat at a Cusco market stall.

We awoke from our final, soggy, overnight camp at 4am for the two-hour trudge through the darkness to reach Intipunku, Gateway of the Sun, the awe-inspiring viewpoint over the sacred city of the Incas. Against a backdrop of towering mountains cloaked in dark-green velvet, we watched the sun slowly drag the shadowed veil from Machu Picchu.

The vivid dawn reflected my current mood: I had left behind the familiar and rediscovered the technicolour excitement of the unknown, of new beginnings. It was the same feeling I'd had on that flight to a new life in Tenerife on June 1st, 1991.

But was my life really that dull that I had to constantly seek change, something better? And would that entail a never-ending cycle of searching for ever greener pastures, of never quite reaching contentment? Was non-stop novelty *really* the only thing that would provide deep satisfaction in my life? The ghost of discontent had haunted my dad. He was always on the move, travelling, seeking new business challenges in new territories, with or without his family. It was a ghost that eventually caused him to take his own life. I needed to be careful.

CHAPTER SIXTEEN

Several weeks after my return, I was still buzzing with it all – the travelling, Peru itself, and the excitement of having spent time in a totally alien jungle environment. Perhaps even more worthy of celebration was the fact that I still had all limbs intact, had no green slime oozing from open wounds and was free of any disfiguring mould clinging stubbornly to my person.

Having said that, Fugly had developed a new habit of excitedly licking one particular spot on my right ankle, punctuated with the occasional sinking in of teeth, of course. It was as though she was gustatorily invested in my adventure through whatever I had inadvertently been branded with on my lower leg.

Above all, I wanted to share my adventure. And then share some more. If Tenerife bus rides had sparked an interest in writing about local travel opportunities, Peru had opened my mind to becoming a globe-trotting travel writer. How hard could it be?

To save having to find other features to fill the gaps between advertorials and ads, Bridget, the editor at *Island Connections*, allowed me to ramble on about my South American experience in many more editions than it deserved. Eventually she slipped into the conversation something along the lines of, 'Perhaps we should wind up the Peru story now.' By that stage I'd already decided that travel writing was what I wanted to do.

When an advertisement on one of the adventure websites I was regularly stalking offered the chance to attend a half-day seminar on how to become a travel writer, I saw this as an open door to a new career. The fact that it was being held in London, some 2,000 miles away, didn't deter me. We still had plenty of money left in the bank from the sale of the Smugglers and I couldn't think of a better way to spend it than investing in my chosen calling.

Joy met the news about my plans with all the calm and conviction of a mother listening to her seven-year-old announce he was going to be an astronaut. 'Great.' She nodded without looking up. 'You'd be good at that.'

We'd both done a series of manual jobs since selling the bar, but Joy was in no hurry to commit to anything long-term. She had been scarred by the demands that bar ownership had made of us both and understandably was happy to remain detached from the rest of the world for as long as possible. It wasn't laziness by any means. If there's one thing Joy isn't, it's lazy. She was brought up knowing that long, regular hours for a decent wage are a fact of life. Her mother, Faith, held down three jobs at once to make ends meet while bringing up five children in a working-class town, and her annual holidays had usually involved working behind the Smugglers bar or washing up in the kitchen. Joy's father had also been a non-complaining grafter, toiling at two full-time jobs to keep the Bolton bailiffs far from their door.

But after a seven-days-a-week, seven-year career in the hospitality industry, Joy was still cherishing her freedom almost as if she were a prisoner newly released from a stretch in jail. Freedom for her meant not being at the beck and call of others. Freedom for me meant not being confined or committed to a life of predictability. I wanted to wake up not knowing what the day might bring or where I might be next month or the month after that. I guess I craved a certain amount of instability.

Travel writing seemed like the perfect fit for someone like me, a quiet talker who preferred to express emotion on the page. I was needy, desirous of praise, acceptance and confirmation of my worth. Needs that may have stemmed from not having had my dad around for much of my upbringing due to similar weaknesses in himself, weaknesses that caused him to put career before family. He'd been brought up alone by my nan, his dad having been killed in World War II when he was only five.

I was aware that my feelings of self-worth and belonging had been slipping since the Smugglers. Becoming a writer and roaming the world would be the perfect antidote. Especially if somebody else was footing the bill.

Six weeks later I took my place in a lecture hall in London along with fifty or so other Bill Bryson wannabees. Though I wasn't quite so enamoured with the author by now, following his absence in Peru. With pens poised above notepads, we waited eagerly for the golden nuggets that would secure us all the best job in the world and everything that came with it – free travel around the globe and our name in lights. Well... print, at least.

It was sure to be a long and arduous struggle; all the articles and books that I'd already consumed made that clear. The seminar itself repeated much of what I had gleaned to date, namely that it was perhaps the hardest niche of any journalism to break into, that you had to find your own voice, and that you needed to show you'd read the publication; in other words, you shouldn't pitch a destination piece to the inflight magazine of an airline that didn't fly there, or suggest an article on an extreme adventure to *Saga*, a publication for those more interested in pension plans and cemetery plots than adrenaline hits. But there were also some useful new titbits that I manically scrawled in my notebook, in particular that the easiest way in if you were new to a magazine was to pitch an idea for one of the regular features such as 'Forty-Eight Hours in [Wherever]' or 'The Ten Best [Whatever] in [Wherever]'.

By the time the third and final speaker had shared their insights, my notebook was half full and my head was humming from the strain of having concentrated so hard. I needed a quiet spot to digest it all.

As the other fifty attendees and I gathered up notes and coats and started to shuffle out, one of the lecturers made a last-minute announcement: 'We're off to the local boozer now. If any of you would care to join us, feel free.'

As I was only in the UK for forty-eight hours, I figured I'd better wring every last drop out of this learning experience. I quickened my step to find out which of the hundreds of London pubs the three founts of knowledge were heading to. Follow the crowd, I figured. But there was no crowd.

A burst of chatter and a comforting amber glow briefly warmed the cold November night as the deputy travel editor of the *Sunday Times* slipped from a dull back street into the Red Lion. I was close behind.

It was six o'clock on a Friday evening and the mock Tudor pub was standing room only. The three lecturers stood near the bar, hands tucked into the pockets of long black coats, the standard uniform of London workers. The editor of *TNT* magazine tried to catch the attention of the bar staff, mouth opening and closing as he failed to get acknowledgement.

Did these bar staff not know who they were? To me they were travel-writer superheroes, living on a different plane to the inebriated office workers around them. Their working space wasn't a cloned compartment in an identikit glass tower. Their office extended from the frozen tundra of the Russian steppes to the backstreets of Calcutta; when they took their seat at work, it could have been in a beach hut in Bali or a penthouse apartment in New York. Each one of them must have racked thousands of miles of foreign travel, with tomorrow always bringing the promise of a new assignment, a new adventure in a new country.

I wanted to tell the bar staff all this, but instead I took my place at the back of a queue three-deep with other mere mortals and waited my turn. As the line dwindled, I found myself elbow-to-elbow at the bar with Max, the deputy editor I'd followed in. We were both in competition to be served first. I knew from my Smugglers days that leaning forward and maintaining eye contact with the person behind the bar was the key to getting the quickest drink.

'Pint of London Pride,' I said as the editor's mouth closed once again in failure. I could feel his eyes boring into the back of my head. 'Can I get you all one?' I braved, turning to face Max and nodding towards his colleagues. The superheroes said nothing. 'I was at the travel-writing seminar.'

Max's expression softened a little. 'Oh, right, sure... thanks. Three London Prides.'

The drinks arrived, and I took a sip. 'Where's everybody sat?'

Max looked puzzled.

'The other attendees.' I'd assumed they'd take over half the pub.

'This is it,' said Max. 'Just you and those three talking to David.'

From a masterclass of fifty people eager to break into one of the most competitive freelance-writing niches, only four of us had seized the golden opportunity to have a one-on-one with industry stalwarts. I was astounded. 'I thought everybody would stalk you back to the pub!'

'We thought so too,' said Max. 'I guess they had trains to catch or something. You're the one from Tenerife, aren't you?'

I was flattered he remembered. The first half hour of the event had been taken up with stand-up introductions from each of us.

'What took you over there?'

I repeated the story that I'd told hundreds of times to customers in the bar, pausing only to accept another pint as the first ran dry. I assumed that, like me, Max was drinking on an empty stomach, and that, also like me, he must have been feeling the full force of the London Pride by now.

I ordered a third and then a fourth as the conversation veered back and forth between stories from the bar and jaw-dropping tales about Max's travels. My confidence had taken a seat in a comfy chair reserved for Dutch courage and I steered the subject back to travel writing. 'Do you get many pitches about Tenerife?' I asked.

'A few, mainly about the nightlife scene, or as a winter-sun hotspot. Nothing unusual.'

I sensed an opportunity and blurted out, 'Can I send you some ideas?'

Despite our alcohol intake, Max hesitated. 'Err... I get at least twenty pitches a day in my inbox, most of them from travel writers we already trust and work with.'

'But Tenerife gets such a bad rap,' I continued. 'It's always the negative stuff that gets printed, about drunken teenagers and foam parties, and the timeshare rip-offs. Nobody prints anything about the other side, the volcanic caves, the subtropical forests, the hidden villages.'

Max nodded in sympathy. 'True, but have you written for anyone else?'

'I've written for a few online publications and I write travel features for the local paper.' I immediately knew that sounded amateurish, but, along with the extra-strong beer, it seemed to do the trick.

'Tell you what, send me some ideas, but no promises. Like I said, this is the big league. Don't try to swim before you can... wait... that's not right. Don't try to walk before you... Well, you know what I mean.'

'I won't, and thanks. Have you got a card?'

He held out a *Sunday Times* business card. 'And do remember everything you heard today. I can't promise anything, but I will take a look.'

I stumbled back out into the chilly evening, my thoughts floating in a bubble of excitement, and also quite a lot of beer.

CHAPTER SEVENTEEN

Back in Tenerife, I continued writing for the local newspaper but with my eyes set on a loftier target. At the time, the *Sunday Times* travel section was running a regular feature called 'Perfect 10', and this is where I aimed to slot my choice of the ten best things to do in Puerto de la Cruz, the city I'd developed a fondness for during my brief visit on my round-island bus journey. There were plenty of obvious things I could write about the place, but, as advised, I needed to surprise readers by including some unexpected things too. After half a day patrolling the streets, I'd made my selection.

I wanted to go beyond the well-known attractions like the Loro Parque wildlife park and the beaches, so I settled on some lesser-known gems. My favourite of these was the naval museum. Some distance from the shops selling local lacework, hidden at the back of the overgrown garden of the eighteenth-century Casa Iriarte, the exterior of this museum looked no more inviting than a decrepit potting shed. Inside, however, visitors were treated to a curious array of maritime knick-knacks exhibited in rooms off a dark maze of creaking corridors. Dusty model schooners, faded photographs of solemn crews, and old manuscripts imprisoned between sheets of Perspex bore illegible captions obscured by long-dead flies. Although some might have seen this scruffiness as simple neglect, life on board a sixteenth-century Spanish galleon would certainly have been no luxury cruise, so what would have been the point of presenting its story in sterile surroundings?

The actual writing of the 'Puerto de la Cruz Perfect 10' took considerably longer than I expected. Twelve days, to be precise. I wrote, I tore up. I restarted, then cast my efforts into the bin. I agonised over the opening paragraph, or 'the hook', as we had been advised to see it, and ruminated on how to end it.

Joy would silently place a succession of coffee mugs on the thesaurus, dictionary, grammar guide and sheaves of notes as I sat staring into the glow of my PC monitor late into the night. And finally I had it, the complete guide to both the obvious and not-so-obvious sights of this northern city.

Joy read it and declared it brilliant. I beamed with pride as I imagined my name immortalised in the Fleet Street hall of fame alongside the distinguished journalists and scholars who had written for the UK's most esteemed newspaper.

I emailed five pages that I hoped was an application for literary fame and fortune, along with the following cover note:

Max,

Over pints of Pride and bucketfuls of Caffrey's, post *TNT* writing seminar, I harangued you into agreeing to look at a 'Perfect 10' piece on Puerto de la Cruz, Tenerife. Well, from the sunny shores of the island they like to call 'trash', here it is.

I continue to fight our corner against the media beasties who paint the island in simple primary colours. There is more here: more subtlety, more sophistication, more sensory feasts than are often served on the wide-screen platter.

Yes, the southern resorts of Los Cristianos and Las Américas are rife with sombreros and sun cream, but the north is a million miles away (well, not quite), and Puerto de la Cruz is the epitome of graceful tourism, a matrimony of serenity and sun in a home of charming character.

The BBC are filming Puerto de la Cruz in early August for part of their *Culture Club* series, so a piece in your Travel supplement around the time of broadcast could be both interesting and timely.

Anyways, enough banging on. Thanks for your useful advice at the seminar, I really got more out of your presentation than from everybody else put together – and that's not (just) a desperate attempt at flattery (I can't afford bribery) – so thanks for your time and I hope we can work together.

Best regards,

Joe Cawley

Tenerife

P.S. By the way, it's your round again!

Now it was just a waiting game.

It took exactly one week of checking my email hourly before a response arrived and what I hoped would be a passport to the best job in the world.

I sat with Joy on the patio. Fugly pawed at my bare ankles but gave up when she could see there was no reaction. I stared at the laptop screen. Joy stared at me.

'Go on then. Read it.'

I opened it with all the care of an archaeologist unearthing a priceless relic. If it was the news I expected, my future career began right now. Not just any career though. A role that was only enjoyed by an elite few the world over. Like a secret agent, I could be one of the strangers on a plane full of holidaymakers, curious stares asking who this mysterious loner could be. I would be the one checking into the hotel with surprisingly little luggage. I would be the one who could pluck a backstreet restaurant from obscurity and set its till alight through a glowing recommendation to hundreds of thousands of readers seeking tips and advice in the Sunday travel sections.

Conversely, I could be the one that put in their place the snooty owner of a pretentious eatery with a few carefully chosen words of caution as to why the reader's holiday money would be best spent elsewhere. I could be that man. And it all started now. With this email. On my laptop. Open.

It began with 'Dear Joe'. A good start.

> Thanks for the 'Perfect 10' – and well done for being the only one to send me something!

OK, let me go in hard here, it'll be easier. This suffers from a bad dose of the twee and cliched. Lots of 'lush', 'boasting', 'treasures', 'claims to fame', 'residing'... fucking sort of stuff that sends me screaming from the room. I want to see really robust writing. What's good about a big penguinarium – the stink, the sight, the sound – WHAT?

Dinner dances and casinos? I can get that in Blackpool.

Oscar Wilde's dad? Umm!

Looking at old pots in a museum: I'd rather get pissed in a swinging pub, you'd rather get pissed in a swinging pub – so write about a swinging pub?

You live there, but you're writing like you saw a travel programme on it last week. It's not rocket science, it's certainly not brochure writing, it's just about writing the stuff people can get excited about. Apply this to all of them and excite me and we might get somewhere!

Sorry. Did say I'd go in hard. Now, that's about £60 of my time – you've got one more go at it!

Good luck!

Max

'Oh,' whispered Joy.

My face glowed pink with disappointment and embarrassment at having got it so wrong. Dreams of joining the big league evaporated.

'At least he took the trouble to write back,' said Joy. 'You told me he said you don't usually get a response unless they like it.'

'True. And I'm pretty sure he didn't like it.' I put the laptop down, stood up and stared out to sea. The world didn't seem like my oyster anymore. It was more like a shrivelled whelk that got stuck in your throat, choking hopes of fame, fortune and foreign adventure.

'But look at this.' Joy's index finger moved across the screen as she read. '"You've got one more go at it."' He's giving you another chance. He must see some potential.'

Such was the darkness of my disappointment, I'd failed to see any glimmer of positivity in his comments on first reading. Suddenly, the flame of hope flickered again. 'Do you think so?'

'Definitely.' She put an arm around me. 'Joe, it's your first attempt. You can't expect to jump from *Island Connections* to the jiddy *Sunday Times* without a little stumbling along the way! Rewrite it and send it back. He's giving you another chance. I think that's brilliant!'

Joy was right. So I did. I attacked my first effort like an assassin. Red ink poured from my pen as I slayed clichés, garrotted brochure-speak and slaughtered a whole battalion of adverbs and adjectives that I'd let invade the page. I had nothing to lose, so I risked bizarre metaphors and threw in as much humour as I could muster.

It took two full days, but when I'd finished, I had become so focused on the fine detail that I couldn't tell if it read better or worse. I knew there was nothing else I could do except risk being rejected again and having to face the sad truth that I'd have to dream of another perfect job.

Joy, of course, told me it was brilliant. But added a pinch

of reality by reminding me that I was aiming rather high for my first pitch to a national newspaper and that I shouldn't be too disappointed if in the end I had to start my ascent up the travel-writing ladder from a lower rung.

I sent it.

> Hi Max,
>
> The bruising is beginning to go down now after the battering you gave me for my previous effort. It's not without a little trepidation and with the satisfactory safety of two thousand miles between us that I send you a rejigged version.
>
> Although not a great lover of pain, I did appreciate the time you gave me in your verbal assault and hope that after reading it this time you won't get the urge to exit stage left screaming obscenities.
>
> Hope it works for you.
>
> Cheers,
>
> Joe

And then I waited again.

CHAPTER EIGHTEEN

Hi Joe,

Something seems to have done the trick – nice work. I've shown it to my boss and she's in agreement. Slight problem in that she's commissioned one of her writers to do Gran Canaria, but we'll see if we can somehow incorporate something from this.

But it'll take a while, so don't hold your breath. Also, I've passed on the piece to the chap who oversees 'On the Cheap', just to see if he's interested in using you.

Well done. If anything gets published, you can buy me that beer.

Cheers,

Max

This time I felt like I'd earned it. I had applied everything we'd learned at the travel-writing seminar and everything that Max had spelled out in his response. I'd found my voice and made the article unmistakably mine. Okay, so they weren't going to use it as they had already commissioned a piece on the Canary

Islands. But he liked it and he'd shown it round, to his editor, to another colleague on the travel desk. Blimey.

I now felt foolish thinking about my first attempt. It was all too clear now how to find your own style and how to avoid being one of the 'brochure writers'. It was also easier. Writing brochure copy was like being a forger trying to recreate a masterpiece: the slightest slip and you'd be found out. Writing from the heart was being the original artist, with nothing to imitate. Yes, you still had to stick to the dimensions required by the client, and the subject had to have been agreed on, but the rest... well, the rest was a blank canvas, as they say. I had suddenly become an artist; not only that, but an artist closer to big-league recognition.

The following day I pushed Max for more, asking if he'd commission another feature. 'No,' was the succinct reply. But his explanation was encouraging. 'You've still got to prove yourself. Send me another article, on spec. If I like it, I'll pass it to the boss and see what she says. No guarantees, but I promise I'll look at it again.'

The *Sunday Times*' new feature, 'On the Cheap', that Max had mentioned was about how to do major cities on a minor budget. The idea was to recommend three or four economical but appealing places to stay and eat, and devise an itinerary that would take in the best sights at minimal cost.

Out of the trio of selections I presented to Max, Florence was chosen as the favourite. I'd never been, but it was on the European major cities map and eventually it would have to be done by someone. Why not me?

I immediately began to research all I could about Italy's Renaissance city. I made lists of the most important sights, worked out when the 'fringe' period fell, just before high-season prices kicked in but when the weather was at its best, and read everything I could about my next destination. The only thing left was to visit the city itself.

At the time, there were no direct flights between Tenerife and Florence. The easiest way to get there was to fly back to the UK and then join a flight from London. The art of 'comping', or asking for complimentary flights, accommodation, car hire and so on in return for a mention in the article, hadn't even entered my head at this stage. Every single expense was borne by my own wallet.

Nor did it dawn on me to contact the tourist board to see if they could help out with any guides, tours or even itinerary suggestions. This was all part of an expensive personal discovery tour.

From nine in the morning until five in the evening I spent four full days tramping the streets of Florence, trying to get a feel for the city. I needed to explore every quarter, test its boundaries and get lost in its maze of unmapped walkways linking one tiny plaza to another.

I watched camera-clicking tourists framing the great works of A-list Renaissance artists. I observed shoppers pumping millions of lire into Armani, Versace and Gucci on the main shopping artery of the Via Roma. And with elbows resting on the ubiquitous checked tablecloths of backstreet trattorias and *osterias*, I became immersed in the storm of breadcrumbs, ranting gabble and waving arms that Italians like to call 'lunch'.

Dining alone was a new experience. Suspicious waiters showed me to the furthest table in the darkest corner, usually sandwiched between a payphone and the toilet doorway. I could feel the stares of neighbouring diners as they conjured reasons as to why I was eating on my own. I hid my self-consciousness in a flurry of note-taking.

Digging out the best accommodation for 'On the Cheap' was the most laborious and soul-destroying task. It required foot-slogging from one end of the city to the other, asking in dozens of guesthouses and pensions if I could see a room. I discovered to my dismay that Florence had an inordinate number of lodgings. They ranged from chic five-star hotels offering front-line views of the River Arno and featuring mints on the pillows, to backpacker hostels offering clothes-line views of the neighbour's smalls and featuring pillowcases on the pillows if you were lucky. I only had three nights to try out three different hotels. Choose the wrong one and it was a night wasted.

In four days I managed to cover most of the major sights, including the Uffizi gallery, the Ponte Vecchio, the painted dome of the cathedral and the statues in the Piazza della Signoria, with just enough time left to dribble ice cream down my T-shirt at Florence's finest *gelateria*, Vivoli.

Back in Tenerife, I tipped all the brochures, flyers and dog-eared notepads onto my desk and wrote up 'Florence – On the Cheap'.

'Brilliant,' was the response from Max. 'We'll buy that and run it next month.'

I'd done it. I was going to have my by-line in the *Sunday Times.* I was an artist with a gallery, not a street busker anymore.

The *Sunday Times* was by far the best-paying travel section of the UK national newspapers at the time. However, as Joy ran through my receipts for plane tickets, accommodation, museum entrance fees and food bills, she announced that I had made the grand total of minus £480 on this one article. But we both realised it was about way more than that: I now had my first foot in the big-league door.

My request for another commission was met with the same response. I still had to prove that these weren't just exceptions. 'Send us another one and I promise to take a look again,' said Max.

And so I headed to Barcelona for another 'On the Cheap'. I absorbed the buzz along La Rambla, Spain's most famous street. I wandered down the narrow alleyways of the Ciutat Vella and Barri Gòtic quarters, where short zigzags of laundry hung between balconies like faded carnival pennants that nobody had bothered to take down. And in the Seu Plaza I watched a flash mob of senior citizens appear from nowhere to form small circles and dance the *sardana*, a kind of Catalan hokey-cokey, before calmly gathering up their shopping bags and vanishing back into the crowd.

Rotterdam was to prove my most challenging, and thankfully final, test. It wasn't a city I would have chosen for a leisure visit, but it revealed a surprisingly beguiling side. If straight-laced industry was its day job, after dark it moonlighted as a pole-dancing ladyboy with a tendency to flash at you then retreat into the shadows.

What I did manage to decipher about that surprising city must have been okay, as within a few days of filing my copy, two things happened in short succession. Both would further boost my confidence and my travel-writing journey.

Firstly, the travel editor invited me to meet her for lunch the next time I was in London. Making another trip to London hadn't even entered my head, but wanting to grab the opportunity by the horns, I made up a reason why 'surprisingly' I would be in the big smoke the following week. Dates were set, flights were booked, and my bank account was lightened yet again.

A reasonably lengthy lunch in a media-flavoured restaurant was followed by a swift pint in a neighbouring pub. I was asked whether I'd thought of moving to London, and then came what I perceived as hints that a more permanent position on the travel desk might be a possibility.

Tempted though I was to swap my place at *Island Connections* for a desk with the big boys at the *Sunday Times*, I politely declined and said I was happy commuting from my hillside home to wherever in the world the commissioning editors might choose to send me. 'Give it some thought,' were the parting words, and I made my way home feeling that somehow, somewhere, I must have cheated to have been virtually offered a position on the biggest travel section in the UK after such a short time in this new trade and following such a steep learning curve.

Back in Tenerife, my head was reeling as I told Joy what had happened; even more so when the phone rang and I received my first non-probationary commission. And as if reeling had no limits, my head was at it again when three days later I received a call from another national paper asking if I'd like to submit some travel story ideas as they'd read my work in the *Sunday Times* and would be very interested in commissioning something from me.

Blimey! The *ST* were sending me to Seville, and now another broadsheet was basically asking, 'Where would you like to go and what would you like to write about?' Blimey again. Where *would* I like to go?

CHAPTER NINETEEN

On our first night in Tejina, I had gazed across the valley appreciatively, relishing not only the view, with the moon casting a pearly sheen over the clusters of cacti, figworts and silver thistle, but also the silence. There was no thump-thump from downtown wafting in and out with the sea breeze, no post-midnight karaoke treats from local wannabes, no scooter boys revving their mobile hairdryers to squealing point. It was quiet, so quiet that for a while it was a little disturbing.

But as I was to discover over the coming days, as soon as the lights went out in the far-off *fincas*, the real sound of rural 'silence' began. This usually started at about eleven thirty, when one particularly gruff bark would signal the onset of that night's canine karaoke. With more verses than 'American Pie', the melee would seem to last forever, peppered with intermittent 'everybody now' choruses from the Tejina de Isora Motley Mutt Choir. The dynamics of the song were admittedly very impressive, dropping to a solitary pining about a long-lost bitch, then rising dramatically in one of those rousing Chas & Dave knees-up party songs.

We were never the only ones to have been disturbed by the dogs. Sometimes a rooster, presumably confused by the rabble-rousing into thinking it had overslept, would burst into alarm mode. Now, if you think the sound of a dozen dogs barking and a slightly demented rooster is as loud as it gets on a country night, you've not heard three cats fighting on your windowsill. On one such night, I feared the pane was going to implode as fur flew, claws slashed and feline obscenities were mashed up with the party sounds from across the way. Flinging open the curtains only caused the decibels to rise; the curling howls of 'It was him', 'It was her' increased, with none of the cats willing to back down despite my flailing attempts to shoo them away.

And if you think the sound of dogs singing, a rooster crowing and a group of stray cats squabbling is as loud as it can get, then you've not heard a goat at full throttle, so full that its voice begins to break, with the vibrato bleating turning to a croaked stutter before crumpling into a goatish coughing fit. That, I can tell you, trumps a party of dogs, a gang of cats and a zany rooster.

Either this welcoming committee disbanded after a few nights or I managed to tune out of the cacophony. Whatever the reason, peace finally prevailed. But there were other perils lurking that Alison had warned us about.

Rigsby himself, for one. His impressive disregard for our safety became something of a menace on two counts. Electrical sockets were jumping out of the wall in various rooms like popcorn in a microwave, some accompanied by a burning odour and plumes of smoke. When we pointed these out on Rigsby's weekly visits, his level of interest barely touched apathy on the concerned scale. Even the blackened walls around the sockets didn't register with him. And when we did manage to get him to do something, rather than bring in professional help, he would attempt to patch up the problem using whatever he had on his person at the time. This could be anything from a roll of toilet paper to a misshapen vegetable. Very occasionally we were lucky enough to warrant a five-minute drive back to his house to pick up a handful of mismatching screws and a hammer. He always managed to curtail the smoking and reinsert the wall socket, but the smell of electrical burning lingered.

The other, albeit lesser, hazard associated with Rigsby was his insistence on keeping us regularly supplied with carrier bags full of produce from his plot of land below the house. Much of what he thrust into our arms with a toothless beam was unrecognisable, though we guessed that most were delinquent relatives of the marrow family. We thanked him anyway, then kept them in the fridge until the weekly purchase of employable vegetables required that his donations be peeled from the bottom of the plastic salad drawer and tossed in the bin. It was only later that we learned we had been right: they were a mixture of *bubangos*, *calabacin* and other vegetables that Canarians use to stodge up stews, soups and casseroles. Despite this, they still had the taste and texture of AstroTurf.

Encouraged by the success of Rigsby's vegetable crop, I decided to dabble with seedlings that would create something a little more conducive to the English palate. If it involved alcohol, all the better. Being a man of the countryside now, I deemed it my duty to produce home-grown wine. How hard could it be? Wild vines grew in abundance in the *barranco*, wrapping themselves around cacti and draping them with bunches of succulent fruit like Christmas decorations. But, try as I might, I could not get my row of vines to produce anything but dry twigs. They clung exhausted to the supporting bamboo sticks, wilting by the day as they waited for death. I watered them, fed them, I even talked to them, mainly about Fugly, but sadly it remained nothing but a one-way relationship.

This new kinship with nature was something we had to get used to. As my experience with the vines had taught me, newcomers couldn't just wade in and tinker with Mother Earth, expecting her to produce on demand. You had to build a relationship. Overall, however, rural life suited us, and we suited it. Seclusion had become more than just a pleasant novelty after the goldfish-bowl existence of El Beril; it was now our preferred lifestyle. But it did have its downsides.

Whereas before we'd had numerous bars, restaurants and supermarkets on tap, in the western hills, to restock at the village shop required a fifteen-minute trek down through the village and a twenty-minute trudge back up, laden with bags.

I suppose it was the equivalent of a convenience shop, except without, well... the convenience. The opening hours put paid to that. Each day had its own schedule. For example, opening times on Monday were ten till six, on Tuesday it was closed all day, and on Wednesday it was open from eight till ten, twelve till two, and then four till five. And so on. Which was all well and good if you had the memory of an elephant. There was also the additional problem that the advertised opening times rarely matched the actual opening times. On several frustrating occasions I marched down to the shop only to find the lights out, the doors closed and a handwritten note informing customers that the shop was currently closed for 'stock-taking', 'circumstances beyond our control' or 'staff shortages'.

The latter I could believe. The shop seemed to be run by two identical twin sisters of remarkably short stature, which I guessed *would* make stock-taking more time-consuming if you couldn't actually reach, or even see, what was on the top shelves. I later learned that one was called Gloria, the other Encarna, though to this day I couldn't say which was which. Both women seemed deeply suspicious of my presence in the shop, despite my efforts to appear friendly and my overabundant expressions of gratitude. In hindsight, as for most Canarians that deal with the British, this probably got on their nerves.

The shop's three dark aisles contained a jumble of groceries placed next to hardware items that in normal shops you wouldn't expect to be shelf buddies. Packets of sliced bread sat next to wooden rat-catchers, and tins of tuna were parked alongside brass rings and other pieces of plumbing systems.

They did have a good fresh bread and cheese section though. Brown paper sacks contained baguettes with aniseed, grainy rolls, and crusty, flour-dusted half-footballs of surprising weight. The glass counter showcased smoked goats cheese, cheese speckled with red pepper, and full rounds that had rinds like car tyres and soft insides that shone like luminous gold. The sisters were very proud of that part of the shop. You could tell from the way they cossetted the produce like adoring mothers.

Not so much pride went into the other parts of the shop, however. There was only one thing that this village supermarket had in abundance. Empty shelves. The proprietors couldn't be bothered, or perhaps couldn't afford, to replenish items that had sold out. Thus many shelves, particularly the top ones, carried nothing but a profuse collection of dust.

There was a nice little bar next door though. Despite the frosty reception I received when I ventured in for the first time clutching a jar of mothballs that I'd inadvertently purchased, it became a regular stop-off for a hot *café con leche.* Sitting outside, watching the delivery men to-ing and fro-ing with all the haste of a funeral cortege, became part of my twice-weekly shopping ritual.

To reach the shop and bar, I had to walk past a laurel-shaded church plaza on my way in and out of the village. It was a thirty-minute workout there and back, plus a ten-minute break in the shop while other villagers caught up with the local gossip courtesy of Gloria and Encarna. But it wasn't just my legs that got some exercise.

The more frequently I made the journey, the more waving it seemed to entail. As a pale-skinned, blonde-ish foreigner in a village of mainly leather-faced residents, it was fair to say I stood out. Particularly as I was male and strolling around carefree during working hours rather than sitting behind the wheel of a tractor or clutching livestock under my arm.

In addition to every pedestrian I encountered, almost every driver waved as they passed. I noticed this happened with particular frequency near the church and I soon got used to shaking an arm and smiling inanely at every motorist. Until I discovered they weren't waving at me. The drivers that I thought were being especially neighbourly had actually been crossing themselves as they passed the church. It was an act of piety, not of neighbourliness. That realisation saved an arm ache or two, not to mention further embarrassment.

Slowly I began to love life in the hills and to loathe the times I had to make the twenty-minute drive south to the tourist area. Entering Playa de las Américas became like driving through the gates of a theme park that I'd outgrown. The high-rise hotels, British bar signs and shops hidden behind racks of beach inflatables felt false, like a lie.

Whereas downtown seemed like a set built for a film, for a specific, profitable and temporary purpose, villages such as Tejina oozed a more permanent vibe. Although some houses, like ours, and Rigsby's own residence, came with no long-term guarantees that they would remain vertical, most were solid structures, not beautiful by any means, but cared for and well tended. There was rarely a day when I didn't see a villager or two sweeping or mopping not only their own doorstep but also the pavement in front of their neighbour's homes.

That would never happen in Playa de las Américas or any of the other resorts, where residents are mostly temporary, with no sense of responsibility for the upkeep or pleasantness of their environment. In the resorts, the hotels, streets, bars, beaches, parks and even people are seen as mere props for the visitor's enjoyment of their holiday. If they get spoiled, damaged or abused, so what? Two weeks later, it won't be their problem. When we had the bar, we were resigned to that. Many times and in many ways we were treated as nothing more than props. We resented that – although I'd like to think that at the time we hid it well.

Now, in this real village, we had the chance to live as locals, to be an *equal* part of the community, not to be used and abused. It hadn't quite worked on my bus journey to integration, but time would tell if it was possible in the long-run.

CHAPTER TWENTY

Much as we loved Tenerife, weekend activities were still somewhat limited, with Spanish still a cerebral challenge. Beach, pool, water park, or a barbecue in the mountains were the principal options. Being an aspiring travel writer, I decided that weekend adventures needn't be confined to our 785 square miles of island. I began to research incredible journeys that could be consumed in just a few days.

Then I had it. Weekend safaris in Africa! After Joy had finished choking on her coffee, I showed her how neatly timed night flights meant that, in theory, we could leave Tenerife Friday morning, have a gander at the big five in Kenya, and still be back in time for Rigsby's rent collection on Tuesday. Joy laughed, Fugly scowled, but the editor loved it. Joy's mockery switched to delirious disbelief when I told her I'd pitched it as a feature for couples and she was coming with me.

Three flights later, Joy and I were dozing on the lawned departure area of Nanyuki airstrip, waiting for a Cessna for the last leg across Kenya's Rift Valley and our weekend safari.

Minutes after lurching off the runway, we saw our first wildlife. Dozens of giraffes strolled gracefully across the plains less than a thousand feet below us. A family of zebras trotted towards a grove of acacia trees, leaving behind a jet stream of flattened red oat grass.

Waiting to whisk us off in a Land Rover when we landed was Gabriel, a Samburu warrior dressed in a red skirt and festooned with green and yellow beads. He was the head guide at our lodge. I was impressed not only by his bold fashion sense but also by his multi-tasking. He managed to avoid every crater in the dirt track while pointing out wildlife hiding behind thorny bushes hundreds of yards away, and there were plenty of both.

Our accommodation was one of five open-fronted cottages on the edge of a ravine through which twisted the Ewaso Nyiro. As with many things in that unforgiving land, a recent drought had reduced the river's strength and drained its spirit. Exhausted from the travel, I immediately spied a herd of scatter cushions and had clear intentions of getting amongst them. But as Joy quite rightly reminded me, on a trip like that, every minute counted when you only had forty-eight hours' worth.

Back in the high-vaulted main building, Gabriel appeared, ready to lead us into the bush. He was still dressed in red robes and sandals. The only concession to safari gear was a rifle slung over his shoulder.

We trudged, head down, in the boiler-room heat. Underfoot, opaque lumps of quartz dotted the red earth like crazy paving. Every few minutes Gabriel stopped, scanned the landscape for danger, and asked, '*Sawa, sawa?*' (Okay, fine?), to which we were instructed to reply '*Sawa*.' After two hours of walking, Joy's '*sawas*' were getting less convincing.

'Another two hours and we'll be there,' said Gabriel, sensing her weariness. Her face dropped. If you remember from her Peru training days, she's not a walker. Gabriel flashed an incandescent smile. 'Just joking. We're here.'

We clambered onto a slab of smooth rock rising above the savanna like a giant anvil. The view made me feel like crying. Groups of zebra, kudu, impala, baboons and water buffalo grazed in the silent green valley below. A red dust spiral danced a slow samba between clumps of foliage before vanishing in the soft breeze. In the distance, the pale silhouette of Mount Kenya was crowned white with snow, a literal icing on the cake of this perfect canvas. It was another moment to savour, albeit one that had involved over 5,000 miles of back-to-back flights.

The following day our itinerary involved 'comfortable camping'. 'No such thing,' moaned Joy. 'Why rough it in a tent when we've got a perfectly good four-poster here?'

The camp had already been set up at a bend in the river, where smooth sandbanks and shiny black boulders provided a 'bush beach' complete with natural diving platforms. Our arrival displaced a party of baboons who were enjoying the late afternoon in an amorous manner that's best left unscripted.

Under a glory of fiery red, we were served a three-course meal with wine and spirits and listened to the croaking of dozens of humongous toads. Eventually, the hypnotic dancing of the campfire flames induced an almighty weariness and we took to our tent with all its luxuries, including a five-inch-deep mattress, crisp sheets and fluffy towels.

At 6am we were woken by shuffling feet outside. Joy said that she'd had the most peaceful sleep, save for the odd camel grunt, baboon yell, hyena laugh, toad croak and insect chirp. Our nocturnal intrusions in Tejina paled in comparison.

A breakfast table appeared outside our tent. The moon was still out, adding a silver glow to the patchwork of pink clouds. While we slurped coffee and munched homemade oatmeal biscuits, the Samburu packed camels and dismantled the previous night's riverside dining table for two.

Two nights proved not nearly enough time for that oh-my-God-I'm-in-Africa feeling to fully sink in, but being able to share the treats of travel writing with Joy was priceless.

As the commissions kept rolling in, I made the decision to leave *Island Connections*. I say, 'leave', perhaps 'was encouraged' is a better way to put it. Frequent requests for time off to travel the world were understandably met with increasing resistance and I was told a decision would have to be made as to whether I gave up the local paper or gave up the trips.

I thought long and hard about it... for around half a second.

Ten days later, I was sitting in a potting-shed-on-legs deep in the southern Carpathian mountains in Romania's Transylvania. I had been shifting my weight from buttock to buttock for over an hour, stubbornly determined to see a bear.

My brief encounters with wildlife in Africa had left me wanting more. More adventure, more travelling, and more wildlife. There was not much to be found in Tenerife – at least not on land, and I could hardly write a feature on our biting-lizard escapades. So, to satisfy my yearning for more wildlife encounters, and continuing the theme of safaris, I'd looked further afield and had come up with the concept of 'European Safaris'. The editors loved the idea. Joy didn't. Having had a taste of the travel-writing life (and perks), she was now beginning to show the first signs of resentment at being left home alone yet again. However, I was now committed. Several days later, I was being paraded through the dusty streets of Zărneşti in a hay cart.

Romania was a surprise and provided the jolt that all travel writers need to produce their best copy. Visually I'd expected monochrome architecture from the seventies, gypsies begging outside scantily stocked shops and the smog of industry choking the towns with dull grey. I was completely wrong. Imagine Switzerland gone bankrupt. You got the orchid-painted meadows, acutely slanting roofs and distant white peaks – only served with a large helping of humility and poverty.

After clearing the ramshackle edge of town, we switched on to a dirt track. Dabs of yellow broom and violet gentian seasoned the flat green pastures between the steep banks of fir and spruce. A stream provided the playground for a pair of storks, while a raven followed our creaky progress all the way to the cabin.

Inside, I was urged to remain silent, but the need to sneeze was as compelling as a fit of giggles during morning Mass. Time plodded on. Then, about a hundred feet away, a dark shadow shifted. Squinting in the failing light, I could just make out the snout of a brown bear sniffing the air for signs of a snack. The huge, slow-moving mass looked as unthreatening as anything in a fur coat with teddy-bear ears could. But then so did Fugly.

Small black eyes locked onto the shed. With head bowed low, it swaggered forward on four huge pads. My mouth grew dry as adrenaline charged through me. Although the timber structure was sturdy, a six-hundred-pound bear could reduce it to matchsticks within a matter of minutes. Fortunately, this bear was only curious, not craving human flesh. I would live to write again.

The trip had been a fantastic experience and was followed by the thrill of seeing my name in a national publication again. Joy's excitement had certainly waned though. Our relationship had become a succession of periods of absence, with me seeing the world and her seeing little more than the back of my head.

CHAPTER TWENTY-ONE

That summer in Tejina was particularly long and scorching. The *calimas* winds were still blowing in dust and extreme heat from the Sahara in September and October. Temperatures in the hills were hitting the high forties and the standing fans we'd bought merely circulated the hot air. There was little we could do but endure the lethargy it produced, and we both yearned for cooler days, missing having the El Beril communal pool and the ocean on our doorstep.

Wanting to banish the blistering heat from my mind, I had pitched a feature on adventurous activities in the Arctic Circle.

'Splendid,' said the editor.

'Blimey,' I responded. Again. It all now seemed too easy.

Aptly, the Talking Heads song 'Road to Nowhere' was playing in my earphones as the plane touched down at Kiruna, 125 miles north of the Arctic Circle. The runway and surrounding area certainly looked like a road to nowhere. The terminal was half buried under drifting snow and all around lay a frozen wasteland spiked with nothing but naked trees.

At the hotel, we were invited to the bar to meet the tour guide and our fellow adventurers. As is the fashion when British travellers meet for the same holiday, conversation turned to how much each of us had paid for the trip.

'Err... I didn't,' I mumbled over a pint of beer when it was my turn for disclosure. 'I'm a travel writer. I'm writing about this trip for one of the UK papers.' In normal holiday circles, the person who paid the least is treated with the same disdain as a person who trumps in a lift. In my case, having paid absolutely nothing, I was treated like a person who had not only trumped in a lift but emptied my bowels and then sung a jolly song about it. I was swiftly ostracised.

I comforted myself with the thought that I wasn't there to make friends, I was there to work and do battle with the elements, my own comfort zone and, unbeknownst to me, a rebellious husky named Ranger.

Apparently, Ranger was a bit of a lady's dog – the Hugh Hefner of Alaskan huskies – intent on making sudden amorous advances towards anything in four legs and a fur coat. This was fine in his own time but not conducive when working as part of a team pulling a slightly overweight journalist across the icy nothingness of Swedish Lapland. The last thing that a slightly overweight journalist needed was to be tipped from his sled onto a frozen lake in front of a group of holidaymakers who had decided that this was the very thing I deserved – even if it was in the name of canine romance.

As it was, Ranger and the other eleven huskies careered off, tails wagging, as my guide, Mats, yelled 'Hike!' to start them pulling. I had quietly hoped for 'Mush!', but you have to go with the flow.

We cut through dog-deep snowdrifts, the eerie silence broken by the sounds of Arctic transport: the clinking of dog-leads, the creaking of birch wood as the sled curved over powdery contours, the crunching of snow under the six-foot-long runners, and the occasional shouts at Ranger to pull his weight. We were the only moving objects in an otherwise inanimate world of faded colour, far removed from the sharp, technicolour wash of Tenerife. Evergreens were dulled with a platinum frosting and the sky, though clear, was a watered-down blue, as half-hearted as the low-lying sun.

With the sled travelling at around ten miles per hour, the wind-chill factor could easily drag the temperature down from minus twenty-four to minus thirty-four, and as Mats cheerfully noted while stuffing another wad of tobacco under his top lip, 'For exposed skin, frostbite is more than just a possibility.'

Back in Kiruna, I defrosted my limbs in the hotel sauna – alone. I briefly flirted with the idea of joining the others in that crazy Scandinavian tradition of snow rolling, but whereas they would be laughing together as a group, I would be enduring the self-torture alone, as an outcast.

Following months of journeying jubilation, this was the first deep-felt unhappiness of my new career, being the object of other travellers' animosity. Although the negative realities of this solitary profession had been apparent to Joy since early on, full realisation had only just set in for me.

CHAPTER TWENTY-TWO

Shortly after my return to Tenerife, Joy and I made an executive decision. It was time to start a family.

Like many childless couples, our pet was supposed to fill the void. If Fugly had been a child, however, she'd have long since been carted off to a juvenile delinquents' centre to test her feline vitriol on those with much sterner attitudes.

Months passed, during which time I accepted travel-writing commissions to Seville, Nicaragua, Croatia, Madeira, Las Vegas and all the other Canary Islands. But while words were produced aplenty, embryonic production continued to be a non-starter.

Tests were taken, results analysed and verdicts given. Namely that there didn't appear to be any sound reason why children weren't forthcoming. After ever more invasive tests, our brilliant GP put a stop to further investigations with the words, 'Sometimes these things happen.'

Over the next twelve months we had many tearful discussions. We decided that adoption might be the best alternative and began to research how to get the ball rolling. Dealings with paper-shufflers during our bar days had prepared us and we had no illusions. If it was near impossible to obtain permission to own a new gas bottle in Tenerife, wow, was it going to be a challenge getting rubber-stamped to adopt a child!

A group of friends were going skiing in Andorra. To cheer ourselves up before the inevitable onslaught of forms, applications and nonsensical interviews, we decided to go with them.

While I struggled with the basics, unable to spend more than a few seconds upright on either the flat or the nursery slopes, Joy skied like she lived – carefree, with great childlike delight and little concern for the consequences. 'Control and balance,' the ski instructor hollered yet again as Joy disappeared down the slopes of Pas de la Casa at full pelt, shrieking, laughing and screaming words of warning to those in her way. I got used to her frequent spills, the orange bobble of her ski hat poking from yet another off-piste drift.

On the third day, however, while I zigzagged gingerly behind, she careered down a red run, hit a bump and completely lost control. As her right leg bounced off the snow, she threw her arms into the air to regain her balance but instead launched herself into a triple cartwheel, landed on her back in the middle of the piste, and then slid corpse-like for well over 500 feet.

A crowd had begun to form by the time I reached her, and I could see the flashing yellow light of an emergency skidoo already racing up from the ski station below. In the twenty seconds it took to get to her, my mind had already decided she had broken her back, her neck or indeed everything. How would we get her home? How would we tell her mum and dad? How would we cope in Rigsby's house now she was paralysed? Would he help us adapt it?

I arrived at the same time as the skidoo medic. His face was set in stone: serious, concerned. It needn't have been. The only thing stopping Joy from getting up was uncontrollable laughter.

'If you're not injured, you must get up straight away,' scolded the medic.

Joy gave him a thumbs-up, still laughing. 'Eeee, jiddy,' she said, 'that was fun!'

It was my turn for a big spill the following day, only I wasn't laughing when it happened. Fresh snow was badly needed in the resort to cover the growing number of ice patches that had appeared. As I skied to a halt to join our crowd after dismounting a ski lift, my left leg stopped but my right didn't.

Those accustomed to the sport will know that having both legs moving in the same direction is preferable to each limb going off and doing its own thing. While my left leg slowly came to a stop, the right found ice and suddenly raced off like a Formula 1 car coming out of the pits. All would have been well if my ski boot and ski had come off as they were designed to do in such situations, but they hadn't. I felt a pop in my leg and fell to the ground in agony. I'd badly torn the muscle in my right calf.

Skiing was over for me. The remaining four days were spent learning how to negotiate frozen roads and pavements with crutches as I made my way to daily physio appointments and the local pharmacy. It was during one of my trips to the pharmacy that something steered me into adding a couple of extra items to my bundle of creams and potions. I gave them to Joy after she returned from the day's skiing.

'Try it,' I said from the settee where I'd whiled away the hours reading and watching the slopes, waiting for her to get back. 'I don't know why, I just have a feeling.'

Joy emerged from the bathroom and we sat in silence watching the dots on the side of the pregnancy-test stick. Nothing. Then the colour changed.

'Is that pink?' said Joy.

I held it up. 'I... I think so. Does it look pink to you?' We exchanged shocked glances. 'Could be the light in here.'

We went to the bathroom and held it under the fluorescent shaving light. Still pink. I followed Joy out of the room and into the hotel corridor. Still pink.

'What do you reckon?' she said, still not convinced.

'It's pink. Try another.' I pulled a second test kit from my pocket.

Joy returned to the bathroom. We sat on the bed and waited again, staring at the little stick. Pink again.

It's at times like these when profound words should toast the beginning of the rest of your life. 'Shit!' was all I could manage. Hands went to mouths. Then the smiles came. Followed by the laughing, and a fist-pumping, goal-scoring, celebratory dance (just me). We were having a baby. I was having a baby. I wanted to be there for every minute, be an amazing dad both before its birth and as our child grew up.

We agreed not to tell any of the holiday crowd lest they try and stop Joy from skiing. On her part, Joy agreed to be a little less kamikaze in her alpine efforts.

My mum became a bawling mess when I told her over the phone. Joy's was more practical in her response. 'You'll have to get rid of that cat now.' We laughed off her comment, but it was a concern. How would Fugly react to a screaming stranger? We'd heard stories of cats less psychotic than Fugly smothering new-born babies out of jealousy. It was a decision we were going to have to ponder carefully over the next nine months.

Fugly was also to undergo something of a change. Strange at the best of times, she had added a new habit to her repertoire of erratic behaviour. One moment she would be lying quietly, plotting her next act of terrorism, the next she would leap off the settee and hare around the living room at full speed. During these sprints, she would stop in her tracks, sit, and seemingly listen for a second, before setting off on another lap of the room.

We became accustomed to these episodes as they became more frequent. Once or twice she would knock over an ornament as she leapt behind the TV, but on the whole little damage was done and we deduced that this new quirk was either attention-seeking or demonic possession. Neither caused too much concern or surprise at the time.

It did, however, when she strolled into the kitchen one morning after having been absent all night.

'Ew! What the...?' My spoon clattered into my cereal bowl. Joy followed my gaze.

Fugly's cute pink ears had been replaced by two blobs of blood-red liver. She threw me the usual disdainful glance, then rubbed her ears back and forth on Joy's bare shins, leaving a wet trail of blood and pus. Joy retched.

We assumed she had been in a fight, but there were no signs of teeth or claw marks anywhere on her white fur. Over the next two days, the fleshy protuberances dried up then scabbed over. On the third day, they turned a crispy black and we rushed her to the vet's.

Skin cancer was the diagnosis. We were told it was very common in white cats as they had little protection on the ears and nose. We were also scolded, quite harshly, I thought, when quizzed as to why we hadn't been applying sun cream to her ears daily.

There was only one thing for it. Her ears had to go. After a couple of check-ups following the amputation, we were informed that the cancer had been caught early and hadn't spread. We were lucky, the vet said, which couldn't be said of Fugly, who now sported knobbly stumps where once her ears had stood. It's safe to say that her new thug look better suited her personality, but any attractiveness that we had imagined as her loving guardians had now been fully quashed. Hideous was too strong a word. But not by much.

The months, then weeks, then days leading up to B-day were passed with controlled trepidation. I really didn't know what to expect. Well, you don't, do you? So when I peered through the viewing window at the row of cots in the Playa de las Américas hospital on October 20th, 2002, any number of emotions were involved in a mass brawl inside my head. Wondrous amazement was trying to free itself from a suffocating headlock of fear, while self-doubt cowered in a corner sucking its thumb. And all because I knew that one of the Jelly-Tot noses protruding from the woollen tea-cup hats and pink or blue bedding was alive because of me.

The nurse glanced up, carefully picked up a bundle of blankets and left the room. The next thing I knew, a tiny face was squinting at me from the folded wool in my arms. I squinted back. Damn, this was something I'd made! Not a something like the Airfix Spitfires that my brother and I ham-fistedly forced together in our early schooldays, though it weighed the same and felt like it too would shatter if dropped. This was... hell, a person that I'd made! Well, Joy and I, to be precise.

I was speechless. Absolutely dumbfounded. How had I made this? There had been no cursing at printed instructions, no stark warnings about using sharp knives without adult supervision, no written cautions about not placing plastic bags over your brother's head. It had been made without fuss or study... but I guess you knew that already. Me? My head was all over the place. If this really had happened, anything was possible.

I softly swept the bobble hat off its head to get a clearer look at its face. And nearly dropped it. A tuft of thick black hair sprang from its head like a rabbit from a hole. Jesus! What the heck was that! The beautiful, priceless gem was crowned with a magnificent Elvis quiff. I looked round to see if anyone had noticed my shock.

The quiff would not be tamed, despite efforts to pat it down with a licked palm. Nonetheless, I was already pitifully in love with this dot of (near) perfection and almost became engaged in a tug-of-war when the nurse returned. I watched her lowering my child back into her tiny bed, silently urging the woman to be so, so careful, and I knew then that life would never ever be the same again.

Four days later, Joy, the baby and I stood outside the glass front door of our house in the hills, waiting to show off the family home to our new arrival. The baby wasn't actually standing, just to make that clear. I'd already decided she was going to be advanced, but not that much!

While Joy was pregnant, Fugly had been strangely serene, as if she knew that changes were a-coming. In the lead-up to the birth, I'd had many a serious man-to-cat conversation, diplomatically explaining that we would both have to adapt, and that the last thing anybody needed right then was trouble. Or claw marks. Fugly listened intently, curled cosily on the back of the settee. Then, without opening her eyes, she flicked out a paw, Freddy Krueger-like.

'Thanks for your understanding,' I muttered, dabbing a sleeve at the bridge of my nose.

Back outside the house, Joy and I looked down at our bundle with all the pride and love you'd expect from new parents.

'How do you think she'll be?' said Joy.

'Fine,' I replied. 'She'll love her little cot and new bedroom.'

'No, I mean Fugly. How do you think she'll be?'

'I've had a word,' I said reassuringly. 'We came to an understanding.' I touched the scab on my nose. 'First sign of trouble and she's on the next bus.' I pushed open the door and paused, waiting for the attack. There was none. But there was the worrying sound of a cat scuttling to gain an advantageous position.

As it was, Fugly avoided the baby at all costs. Perhaps my words of warning had hit home. More likely she was in observational mode, stealthily watching and planning the best way to do battle. So far, so good, but time would tell.

CHAPTER TWENTY-THREE

I don't know why, but I thought that the paperwork involved when a new person checked in to this world would be easier to get through than other bureaucratic demands in Tenerife. In the normal scheme of things, the island's administrative department would surely try to make it easier for mothers, whether single or with a partner, now that they had the trifling matter of keeping a baby alive to add to their day-to-day duties – wouldn't they? They would give consideration to those who had just endured possibly the most painful and traumatic ordeal they would ever experience. They would go out of their way to provide sympathy and support to those mothers who might still be suffering mentally or physically, to those finding it difficult to walk or simply unable to find any spare time for crossing 't's and dotting 'i's.

So what does the Tenerife state department do? It obliges all new mothers to present themselves at the local registry office within ten days of giving birth. Not only that, they have to bring a baby with them, preferably their own. On top of that, only fifty mothers can be seen per day, and to be one of those mothers, you have to make sure you're in receipt of one of the first fifty tickets handed out each day.

And how do you ensure that you're the fortunate holder of said golden ticket? Armed with a baby and a bundle of paper-work, and walking like you're astride an invisible horse, you have to queue up at 7.30am with enough steely determination to ignore the unfriendly, officious and probably childless desk clerk, who displays all the empathy and understanding of a serial killer.

And do you think they provide seats for all the queuing mothers, half dead on their feet and carrying eight-pound bundles that leak vomit, pooh and dribble? Don't make me laugh.

Thankfully, Joy was relatively mobile despite having been stapled back together following an emergency caesarean, and she had an other-half with the flexibility of being self-employed and who happened to be between overseas assignments.

After taking a ticket from the dispensing machine, we stood with the fifty or so other new parents waiting to register their new arrivals. But for the absence of a 120-beats-per-minute soundtrack, we could have been in a disco. Some mothers jigged up and down, trying to soothe restless babes in arms. Others swayed gently from side to side, partly to lull little ones on the verge of hysterics and partly to provide the sort of reassuring comfort self-administered from within padded cells.

Naturally, the number on our ticket and the digital count-down clock were miles apart. We spent our time comparing babies. Clearly ours was the most beautiful. None of the others had such a distinguished Elvis quiff. '*Qué preciosa!*' the other parents would squeal, followed by a universally understood 'Oh!' when her hair quiff sprang to life.

After a couple of hours' standing, shuffling and swaying, we carried our bundle to the lady at the desk. Understandably, she was a little child-weary by this stage and could manage only a conciliatory grunt of a greeting.

She pulled back the blankets shielding our baby's face then presented us with a form plucked from an extensive selection of stacks. I presumed that if we had been carrying a bag of carrots under the blankets, she would have nonchalantly slipped us a form for that instead.

We began to fill in the form at the desk, but she shooed us away and attended to the next person. After completing the paperwork as best we could, there didn't seem to be a process for re-joining the queue to hand it in. Like the others, we stood with papers raised in one hand, baby held in the other, waiting for directions. None came. Were we supposed to get another number and queue again? Was there another desk we had to go to? Did we need to strip naked and run riot to get attention? It crossed my mind. Instead, we followed the lead of the Canarian mothers and pushed in front of those on the first, ticket-wielding leg of this joyless odyssey.

Despite much tutting from behind, our form was grabbed by the spectacled lady. She scanned it, crossed out Joy's surname, peeled off one of the three copies, gave it to us and moved on to the next person. We hung around at the desk until she gave us that impatient 'Why are you dawdling?' glare, then left.

It was only afterwards that we discovered she had personally had a hand in naming our child 'Molly Blue Cawley' rather than the double-barrelled 'Molly Blue Cawley-Liddell' that Joy and I had negotiated with each other.

Back at home, more trauma was waiting. Fugly had ceased her attacks on me. We were worried. From her favoured vantage point on the back of the settee she barely lifted a head as I came within striking distance. I walked back and forth a few times just to check.

'Maybe she's finally accepted you,' said Joy.

But I sensed there was more. There was – in the kitchen, on my side of the bed (naturally), in the garden. In fact, half a dozen small pools of yellow bile and vomit dotted our home. The following day we bundled all four members of our family into the car.

While cat psychiatrists were short on the ground in Tenerife, regular vets were not. Perhaps the Canarian predilection for human hypochondria was apparent in the island's wildlife too. Our vet of choice hadn't seen our cat for a while. That did nothing to dampen the look of fear on her face when she saw Fugly peering from within a McCain's Frozen Chips box.

'How is she?' she said from a good distance.

'Not very well,' replied Joy forlornly. 'She has yellow sick.'

'No, I mean is she still...' She raised her fists like a boxer. 'You know... violent?'

We both nodded apologetically. The vet sighed and pulled a pair of industrial gauntlets from a metal drawer.

She ordered me to hold Fugly still, keep her calm.

'Me?' I said. 'Calm' was not something I was good at instilling in her.

Joy volunteered. As the vet approached the stainless steel examination table, Fugly began to growl like the girl from *The Exorcist*. I'm sure I heard the vet whimper.

'You have hold of her, yes?' she asked.

Joy nodded.

But as soon as the vet came alongside Fugly, the fight in her went. 'Oh,' said the vet, 'I can see she's not well at all.'

Blood samples were taken, internal organs felt, and vaccinations administered. All accompanied by nothing more violent than a baritone gurgle and a token baring of teeth. But the vet looked worried. 'I think we need to have a look inside, an X-ray. Her liver is swollen.'

For the X-ray, Fugly had to be put to sleep, which meant that she would be overnighting at the surgery to recover from the anaesthetic.

We returned the next day, and so had Fugly's temper, which made us happy. The vet was not so cheerful. I noticed a plaster on the back of her hand, where yesterday there had been none. But the injury was not the only thing she was concerned about. 'The cancer has spread,' she said sadly. She waited for the significance of her words to sink in before continuing. 'It's in her liver, her spleen, and I think it's started in her lungs.'

Joy and I just looked at each other. Joy spoke first. 'Is there anything you can do? Any treatment she can have?' The words were said in a low, desperate whisper.

The vet shook her head.

'How long do you think she has?' I asked hesitantly.

The vet sighed. 'Hard to say. Weeks. Months. Possibly a year. It depends how fast it spreads from now on. She's a fighter. That's a good thing.'

'Is she in pain?' asked Joy.

'Not now. I can give you some drugs. That will help.'

We wrestled Fugly back into the box as gently as two people wearing elbow-length gauntlets could manhandle a writhing mop of anger.

At home, she darted from the box and hid under our bed, hissing if we even dared to venture past the bedroom door, and there she stayed for almost a week.

In the morning, Joy fed Molly. She'd finally managed to get us into a clockwork routine of feed, sleep, feed, sleep at more or less regular intervals. When either was needed, Molly let us know with air-raid-siren wails, demanding immediate attention. Then, while our daughter guzzled sleepily, I packed for Alicante, where I'd be researching one of a series of features I'd been asked to write for *Homes Overseas* magazine.

The commission required me to make a four-day trip to the mainland to write about property hotspots. Walking out of the house that day felt different. It was the first time since Molly had been born that I'd had to go away. As I waited for take-off at Tenerife's north airport, there was none of the usual excitement at the prospect of exploring a new destination. The anticipation of discovery was absent; in its place was an empty hole and nagging guilt that I was not with my family.

By the time I touched back down in Tenerife, I'd made the

decision. I would complete this series of six commissions for *Homes Overseas*, then finally and fully quit travelling to be with Molly and Joy.

My dad had often been absent during my childhood, and in my mind I'd vowed not to do the same. I had a family, a duty, but more than that, a desire to do my best, give my time and be there for my daughter as much as possible.

I remembered clearly the infrequent occasions when my dad had been at home for any length of time. After he moved to America, my brother and I would sometimes go and visit him there. I could still recall the cycle of emotions: the excited anticipation, the thrill of being together again, with all that love and bonding, then the dread as departure day loomed and we began counting down the hours, and finally the heartbreak of watching him walk away. Coming home from those reunions was always painful, with me spending a lot of time alone in my bedroom, in tears and desperately sad. I was a young boy. I needed my dad. I needed the stability of a permanent father-figure, a hero, even. I did not want to put my daughter through the same cycle.

I also had the responsibility to provide, and unfortunately this meant I would have to find something else that would keep the money flowing in. *Island Connections* seemed like a step backwards, but it was possibly the only writing job I could get in Tenerife. Having written for just about every national newspaper in the UK, I really didn't want to go back to rough translations of Spanish articles and fawning features on local politicians. But the job pool wasn't exactly awash with alternatives.

With me choosing to be a stay-at-home dad, Joy secured a part-time job at a local travel company in the Patch area of Playa de las Américas. It had been a while since she'd had a role outside her own family. It was also an office staffed entirely by women, so the gossip was bound to be good.

My days, meanwhile, consisted of working on the odd Tenerife feature while Molly slept, then bouncing her on my knee as we sang along to the *Tweenies*, *Peppa Pig* or the *Teletubbies*. A macho culture still thrives in the rural reaches of the Canary Islands, much as it does in mainland Spain. Women have *their* roles, men theirs. Usually there isn't much crossover, especially when it comes to childcare. It was considered a bit of a novelty in Tejina when a dad showed up in daylight hours with a baby strapped to his chest.

As soon as I entered, the supermarket sisters would whisk Molly away, singing squeaky Spanish baby songs to her from one of the dark recesses while I filled my basket. In the coffee shops too, the staff would invariably kidnap my daughter and take her behind the bar or into the kitchen. On several occasions I had to ask for my bill *and* for my child back.

However, as much as I loved our father–daughter time, Joy's part-time wage along with my infrequent local travel commissions weren't enough to stop us having to break into our savings every month, especially with a new arrival to feed, clothe and keep in toys. I needed to start earning some regular money that would still give me the freedom to work from home around Molly's demands.

CHAPTER TWENTY-FOUR

Fortune struck again a few months later when I was asked to contribute to *Living Tenerife*, a glossy lifestyle magazine that had recently launched. Set up as something of a diversion by the director of a UK newspaper group, the monthly magazine was only two editions into its lifetime and was being run from the cellar of a villa in Callao Salvaje, a coastal community just fifteen minutes from Tejina.

The publication showed great promise but clearly needed direction. Although I was no expert, my experience as a freelancer with the top newspapers and travel magazines had given me a certain amount of insight and I could see it badly needed help with its structure, style and editing.

My one article turned into two, then four, then five, oh... and would I mind spending some time in the office proofing the pages before the third edition went to print. The managing director took me to one side and asked if I'd be interested in becoming the editor as well as the principal contributor, working from home two days a week.

Four months later, the UK owner ploughed in some extra funding, the magazine moved into a new office, and a full-time contract was provided for me, a graphic designer, an office manager and a sales manager. I was also allocated an editorial budget for commissioning writers and photographers. Other duties included coming up with monthly editorial schedules, developing new ideas for features series and working with the graphic designer on a new look for the magazine.

It was exciting and varied work and as I was still contributing articles it also gave me the opportunity to try new experiences in order to write about them – windsurfing, scuba diving and sailing among them. I introduced a new monthly section on Tenerife's best spas, and partly due to the lack of editorial staff, but mainly because I was the editor and thus could choose the perks, I was invited to experience the delights of soft-handed caressing and the finest skin products money could buy.

On one such occasion, wearing nothing but paper pants and an air of curiosity, I was painted from head to toes in rich, smooth chocolate. I looked like a loose-limbed éclair.

'What does it taste like?' I asked my decorator.

'Chocolate,' she replied, rather obviously.

After scooping a fingerful off my stomach, I couldn't disagree. It was essentially just like edible chocolate but without the butter and was supposed to stimulate mood-elevating endorphins and leave you feeling rejuvenated.

A lid was pulled down, encasing my torso like an iron lung. I was now a chocolate filling with a hard coating – an M&M perhaps. With just my head protruding, I watched the lights dim and listened to a succession of tinkly tunes and chants while the sweet stuff worked its magic. Inside the oven, I was steamed for twenty minutes. The aroma of warm chocolate was pleasant at first, but like when you turn immediately to the second layer of treats in a box, it soon brought on a touch of nausea.

Next on the menu of the day was a wine bath. Alleged therapeutic benefits included improved circulation. Regardless of whether that was true, any detox treatment that involved copious amounts of wine was okay by me, even if the red stuff did remain on the outside.

The tub that me and my disposable knickers were invited to sit in was no Armitage Shanks, toe-stuck-in-the-tap bath. A contoured oyster shell provided semi-horizontal relaxation in all the right places, while underwater jets gently manipulated every muscle. Again, thanks to the soft lighting and ambient piano notes, it was inevitable that sleep would follow. I had found my new calling – spa writer! Throw a litre of local red into the formula and the pearly gates had never seemed closer.

Being at the helm and having control of the magazine's aesthetics and content was a new experience, but so was having to work hours that someone else dictated. I was also expected to attend press conferences, society events and dinners with local dignitaries, which meant I wasn't returning home until late most days.

I would try to include Joy in my evening commitments, but she wasn't keen. Having at last fully overcome the aversion to people that had plagued her in the immediate months following our bar sale, she was now itching to be sociable, but only with those *she* chose. Our bar days had shown us what a mixed bag of reprobates mingled with the decent folk in Tenerife. Worse than the pathological liars, fantasists and downright dodgy were the faux elite, the British snobs whose colonialist attitudes clung to them like colostomy bags.

Former Smugglers patrons and anyone who has met Joy in Tenerife can probably attest to the fact that she's one of the friendliest, warmest and most amenable people on the planet. But put her anywhere near sharp instruments and island snobs and she'd happily embed one in the other. So it was no great surprise that when I invited her to an expats' Wine Society do, she gave me a look that you rarely see outside maximum-security prisons.

However, hotel stays were her weak spot and subsequently proved to be the tipping point. An all-expenses-paid night in a five-star convinced her to put aside her loathing – and any sharp objects – and agree to accompany me. In hindsight, perhaps it would have been better if we'd both declined the invitation.

The evening started off well enough, with chocolates on the pillow, cava on ice, and beds sized for a party. It was the actual do that flattened the occasion.

Joy and I were seated at one of a dozen round tables in the hotel ballroom, sandwiched between a balding man in dandruff-speckled tuxedo and a starched lady with the steely glare of Margaret Thatcher and the pinched expression of an involuntary lemon sucker. She looked Joy up and down. 'Where does one come from?' she asked.

'Bolton,' said Joy, in the strongest Lancashire accent she

could muster.

'Oh,' said the lemon sucker, unimpressed. 'Sounds frightful.'

I moved the cutlery out of Joy's reach. 'Have you travelled far?' I asked the man with dandruff. He nodded sagely. But that was it.

I nodded back.

A portly man at the head table tapped a glass with his butter knife and stood up. Glancing around the room, I could see that Joy and I were half the age of every other diner.

'Ladies and gentlemen,' began the orator.

'Shit!' said Joy.

I turned around. She had spilled a full glass of red down her new cream dress, which was now crimson, the same as her face. The rest of the table looked on. Dandruff man nodded sagely. Nobody offered a napkin, or any other help.

'Dab some fizzy water on it,' I whispered.

'Dab! I need to pour the whole flamin' bottle over me. I'm covered!'

'Shall we go back up to the room, try and get it off?'

Joy nodded. I gave her my jacket to hold in front and we apologised our way out of the room with the orator's amplified quip filling the ballroom with chortles. 'Early night for that lucky boy, eh?'

Joy had no other dress, and it was futile trying to clear the wine stains. 'You go back down,' she said. 'I'll stay up here and watch telly.'

I headed back down, and, mellowed by the wine – on the inside, rather than the outside this time – I endured the night and all its my-boat's-bigger-than-your-boat boasting and general snobbishness.

The owner of the magazine had asked me to befriend the guest of honour, the British consul. 'It would help to have friends in high places,' he'd said. I duly sidled over to the consul and bagged the seat next to him at the first opportunity.

He was actually a very interesting character, slightly younger than the rest and full of amusing anecdotes about life in Scotland and his short time getting used to Tenerife. I felt we got along very well and was pleased with myself at having accomplished my mission.

'I expected a consul to be more... stuffy,' I said as we toasted our new friendship over crystal tumblers of fine single-malt whisky.

'So did I,' said the consul. 'He seems okay, though.'

I paused, glass in air. 'Who?'

'Peter, the consul.' He pointed his glass at a man saying his goodbyes at the ballroom door.

I shook my head and blinked hard. 'So you're not the consul?'

'Me? Hell, no. I'm a teacher at the international school. I don't think they'd want me in the diplomatic corps. Not with my background!'

And there began another round of stories and whiskies, which continued well into the night and then straight into one of the most horrendous hangovers I'd ever experienced. Still, the hotel bathroom was nice.

I guessed that all this networking for business would be required in pretty much any serious career in the UK, but working so hard for somebody else was beginning to grate. Added to that, my aim to be around for Molly as much as possible was being thwarted by the long and irregular hours demanded of a magazine editor.

The seeds of change had sprouted again. And unbeknownst to either Joy or me at the time, they weren't the only seeds that were growing.

CHAPTER TWENTY-FIVE

One of our regular pages in the monthly *Living Tenerife* magazine was reserved for reviewing books about the island. Or at least that's how it started. We soon discovered that English-language books about Tenerife were severely limited in number. There were the usual walking and travel guides, plus the odd tome about the wheezing gentry who'd frequented nineteenth-century Tenerife to take advantage of the island's climate.

To continue the feature, we were going to have to broaden our horizons a bit. At first we extended the remit to include books about any of the Canary Islands, not just Tenerife; when those ran out, we accepted any books that contained even a passing reference to the archipelago. Finally, we allowed anything that included sun, sand or sea either in its title or in the image on the cover.

The postman often brought books from small presses with covering letters requesting that we write nice things about their author's words. Very occasionally I would receive a preliminary phone call from the publicity department of said publishing house. It was during one such call that an opportunity arose, an opportunity that would change my career path again.

I'm a great believer in making your own luck. That's not to say luck never visits uninvited. It does, and it's during those unexpected house calls that you need to sit luck down, offer it a nice cup of tea and make polite conversation until you find out just why luck pressed your doorbell instead of your neighbour's.

Put a less cosy way, it's all about recognising an opportunity, grabbing it unceremoniously by the *cojones* and only releasing it if you're sure it can bear no fruit.

'Hello, this is Amy Cartwright from Made-Up-Name Publishing House. We have just published a wonderful book, *Random Waffle from an Ex-Fleet Street Hack*, by the very talented author, Notsaying Hisname. Have you heard of him?'

'Can't say I have.'

'*Pretentious Book Title*? Flowery Tome? "The Never Heard Of It" series?'

'Nope. Sorry.'

Pause. 'Anyway, could I send you a review copy?'

'Well, to be honest, we try to only feature books with a Canary Islands angle, or at least a vague association.'

'Oh, okay. Never mind. Thanks for your time.'

And then I blurted out a blatant lie.

'I've written a book.'

'Oh. Have you,' sighed the voice.

'Yes. It's very good.'

'Is it *really*!'

'Can I send it you?'

'Err... I guess so.'

She gave me the address of the commissioning editor and I promised to forward my book as soon as possible. Brilliant! A foot in with a publisher. I was feeling very pleased with myself despite there being one tiny detail absent. I didn't have a book.

What I did have were copious notes from our bar days, scrawled in a dog-eared journal and on loose pieces of paper, serviettes and the backs of peeled beer mats. I couldn't remember why I'd written so many things down, except that it probably provided some sort of cathartic relief from the frustrations of bar life. By putting it down on paper (or beer mat), I could better process the idiocy of some of our customers and resident expats. My run-ins with the gun-toting, the deranged and the merely daft-beyond-belief were not cruel tricks of my overworked mind and exhausted body – my scribblings proved that they had really happened.

When we'd cleared out all our belongings from the bar after it was sold, I had herded these stray notations into a manila folder. I also had a vague notion that one weekend when I was bored I'd assembled them into some kind of order in what could loosely be described as three chapters. What I couldn't recollect was what I'd done with them next.

Thanks to the zealotry of the island's bureaucrats, we had amassed stacks of paperwork, all neatly suited in matching manila then shoved into any spare space or box in our tiny apartment. I distinctly remembered Joy commanding that we be brutal with what was kept and what was discarded from our lives, a sacrificial cleansing of our past, a past that had broken our relationship (nearly irreparably) and challenged us with one nonsensical calamity after another.

Then I remembered. We had lit a bonfire on the waste ground. Lots of smoke. Lots of manila. Damn! I was pretty sure all the folders had been cremated, which meant no book, no notes and no authorial fame. I would have one more look when I got home.

At home, Fugly had gone AWOL. She'd not been seen since the day before. We were both beginning to get worried.

'Have you checked outside?' asked Joy.

There weren't many hiding places around the cacti, concrete or volcanic gravel, but our house in the hills did come with a garage. When I say garage, I mean a corrugated roof propped up on three sides by a medley of stones and breeze-blocks. It had become the dumping ground for anything that had even the remotest possibility of being needed in the future, such as plastic sheets, dusty shot glasses and bits of string.

Being male, it didn't take much to distract me from my initial purpose and I began to flick through the reams of paper and box files containing bar invoices and receipts, instruction manuals for electronic equipment we no longer owned, and legal documents for a car we had sold over three years ago.

Of more interest was a shabby cardboard box that contained a manila folder. I was even more impressed that the manila folder held an assembly of pages that looked suspiciously like a work-in-progress.

I sat on the concrete floor and began to flick through the papers detailing stories about Fugly's predecessor, Buster the dog-cat, our trauma with the squatters, the numerous dealings with ridiculous bureaucrats, and the catastrophic bar fumigation that temporarily wiped out our entire customer base.

I wondered what had happened to people like Duncan from the market. Was he still alive? Was he still being chased and teased by Bolton's bullet-headed bullies? What about Pat, our ex-boss on the fish stall. Was he still flogging the same 'lemsy' (smelly) chicken and dubious trays of fish at three for a fiver?

And Friedhelm, our loyal German patron with perennial 'big problems'. Was he still visiting brothels, choking on Marlboros and sitting forlornly at a barrel table in another bar? If so, I hoped they were treating him well.

Some people had undoubtedly moved on. Things changed. Blimey – our lives certainly had. Now we were three. Three and three quarters, if you counted the bits of Fugly that hadn't been amputated.

I'd also finally found my mojo, via writing – not the typical career progression of a pub landlord, it had to be said. But it was something I knew I was going to be doing for the rest of my life. It was *my* thing.

In my office the next day, I typed the chapters into a Word document and emailed them to the publisher. I then called Joy at the house to see if Fugly had shown up. She hadn't. Joy had scoured the wasteland below our house, but there was no sign.

Three days later and we'd come to the sad conclusion that Fugly had taken herself off to die. Apparently, it's not uncommon for animals to do this. Disregarding the comforts of home, they prefer solace and isolation when the end beckons. Despite her flaws, and this natural urge, Fugly was still part of our family and the thought of her dying alone and in pain was difficult to accept.

More demands were being put on me at work, and although the money was okay, I didn't believe I was being paid enough for the hours, responsibility and time away from my daughter. Molly was developing without me. That had definitely not been the plan. With Joy still working part-time, our daughter was spending most of her days at a childminder's. There was no doubt she was happy, but it felt like we weren't giving her enough of ourselves. I summoned all my courage and asked for a pay rise. The management summoned all their authority and turned it down.

I needed time to think, a break away with Joy. Although the travel commissions had stopped, I had one more trip to take for the *Sunday Times* that I'd committed to several months earlier. It was a piece on the carnival in La Palma, one of the neighbouring islands. It involved a one-night stay and Joy was going to come with me.

It would prove to be a real strain leaving Molly overnight with the childminder, but the time away would give us the chance to think, regroup and figure out how to get our family life back on track.

CHAPTER TWENTY-SIX

Canarian celebrations are often outlandish affairs, but none is more bizarre than *carnaval* on La Palma. For most of the year the islanders quietly work the green upland terraces for bananas and tobacco. But in February they head down from their hillside hamlets to the pocket-sized capital, Santa Cruz, where on Carnival Monday the colonial-style town turns into a war zone.

On this day the island goes pale beneath an orgy of hand-to-hand combatants employing nothing more sinister than squeezy bottles of baby softener. Over 10,000 pounds of ammunition is discharged in powder-puff clashes during the *batalla de polvos de talco* (talcum powder battle). A couple of pounds had just been dumped on our two heads.

Unlike in other wars, each round of artillery fire was followed by friendly hugs and good-humoured apologies. It was during these interactions that my suspicions were raised. I could see Joy squirming with each cuddle.

'You okay?' I asked through blinking, minstrel eyes.

'My boobs really hurt,' said Joy, wincing.

'You pregnant again?' I said through the melee, laughing.

Joy's face was serious. 'I think I might be.'

Before I could respond, a thunder of drumbeats exploded around us and we were swept along, separately, in a tide of revellers. A band of forty drummers had struck up a Brazilian beat and the powdery fog increased proportionately with the cacophony, talc bouncing off drum skins with every forceful accent.

We came together again at a pharmacy doorway, where a middle-aged English couple were jigging awkwardly to the beat of the approaching band. The husband 'danced' into the street to allow us to pass into the shop. 'Derek, come over here, out the way,' called the woman. But the man in pressed slacks was trapped in the human current. The samba beat erupted around him and he must have just caught sight of a rush of white faces before he looked up, spluttering in a cloud of perfumed dust. 'Derek!' admonished the woman. 'I wanted you to wear those trousers tomorrow.'

Joy and I found a seat at one of the pavement bars. Next to us, a group of sun-wizened musicians under south-sliding panamas looked like they'd peaked too soon. The maracas player was doing his best to join in the rhythm. The other members had long since decided that boisterous singing was the best they could manage in their inebriated state. The louder they sang, the more talcum powder was hurled their way, until even the lame vocalising spluttered and coughed to a halt.

'Do you really think you're pregnant?' I asked.

'I dunno. I just feel... weird. Been feeling like this for a few days.'

As the procession approached, we realised that conversation was futile. Making eye contact with anyone on the street was a declaration of war. It wasn't long before I felt as if I was back in the chill of my nan's bathroom, aged three, choking in a blizzard of Woolworth's finest during a liberal dousing with talcum powder

After an hour or so of indiscriminate attacks, people, palm trees and road were as white as the smallholdings stretching up the slopes to the volcanic peaks. Like a Christmas scene from Dickens, flaking doors and low-hanging dark-wood balconies bore snowball scars, and loose powder formed drifts on windowpanes.

We decided to dip out and watch the rest of the mayhem from our hotel. As Joy went to the bathroom, I set chairs up on the balcony and checked out the minibar.

'Rum and Coke?' I shouted, just as Joy came out of the bathroom holding the pregnancy tester.

'Better make it just Coke,' she said with a smile.

Back at home the following night, we discussed the impending arrival and how it would affect our current situation. As we were doing so, we heard a familiar squeak. We both stopped talking and raised our heads like meerkats.

The squeak was repeated. I slid open the patio door and looked down. It was like Groundhog Day from three years ago. At my feet, a dishevelled white cat looked up. It was Fugly, still alive after being absent for six days! We were both ecstatic.

The birth of Molly, the impending arrival of our son, Sam, and, in an indirect way, Fugly's reappearance, finally made me realise what I'd been chasing all of my adult life. It wasn't really adventure, or change or praise. It was a return to the concrete stability of family, my own family. Just like Tenerife, I too had now officially passed from reckless adolescence into adulthood.

That year, 2004, would see the birth of our beautiful son, Sam. But that was not the only new beginning. The publisher who I'd spoken to on the phone four months earlier called me at my office the day after Carnival. She'd read my three chapters, and that was enough to convince her that she wanted to buy my crazy scribblings about moving from Bolton fish market to a bar in the sun. She asked if I could send the rest of the book. I confessed that what she had was all that had been written.

'Oh,' she said, disappointed.

I felt the publishing deal slipping from my hands. 'But the rest is all planned out, so it wouldn't take me long to finish it,' I lied.

'How long?'

'Nine months?' I figured if the advance was enough, I could spend the next nine months working from home, which would mean I'd be released from the shackles of office work and free to spend time with Molly, and for the birth of Sam.

She hesitated. 'Okay, fine. Have the rest of the manuscript to us in six months and we have a deal. I'll email a contract with details of the advance and royalties we'd like to offer. What's the book called, by the way?'

'I'm not 100 per cent sure yet, but I think it's going to be called *More Ketchup than Salsa.'*

'Love it,' she said. 'Perfect.'

Have you seen my photos from the Smugglers days?

If you haven't, go to my website below, leave me your name and email address, and I'll send you some.

I'll also add you to my subscriber list and let you know when my next book is out.

There'll be no spam. I promise.

www.joecawley.co.uk

About the Author

Joe Cawley is a full-time writer, now living in the hills of Tenerife with his family and an assortment of other wildlife. He's the author of More Ketchup than Salsa, Even More Ketchup than Salsa, and Less Ketchup than Salsa, and the co-author of Moving to Tenerife, a useful guide for those determined souls who haven't entirely been put off living in Tenerife after reading this and his other titles.

When not writing or editing, he's often found talking to his dog, chickens, goats, guinea pigs, turtles and fish.

Find out more about Joe and his other books at www.joe-cawley.co.uk. Joe would be mighty pleased if you joined him and said hello on the following social media channels:

Twitter - @theWorldofJoe

Facebook - Facebook.com/JoeCawley

If you'd like to get in touch, please send a message to writer@joecawley.co.uk with any comments, opinions, requests or general waffle. Writing can be a lonely chore and any contact with the real world is much appreciated.

Joe is also the editor/owner of the online MyGuideTenerife, so if you're visiting the island and what to know what to see/do/visit, you'll find all you need to know right there.